Cooking Under Pressure

by the same author

THE HOSTESS COOKBOOK (Angus and Robertson)

TRADITIONAL ENGLISH COOKING (Angus and Robertson)

PRESSURE COOKERY (Odhams Press)

TIME SAVING COOKING (Odhams Press)

FOOD, FLOWERS AND WINE (Odhams Press)

THE FLORAL ART BOOK OF REFERENCE (Pergamon Press)

MR AND MRS CHARLES DICKENS ENTERTAIN AT HOME (Pergamon Press)

COOKING UNDER PRESSURE

Helen M. Cox

FABER AND FABER LIMITED
3 Queen Square London

First published in 1977
by Faber and Faber Limited
3 Queen Square London WC1
Printed in Great Britain by
Latimer Trend & Company Ltd Plymouth

ISBN 0 571 10825 3
(hard-bound edition)

ISBN 0 571 11103 3
(Faber Paperbacks)

Contents

THE RECIPES

THE WHY AND HOW OF PRESSURE COOKING

1. A Benefactor in the Kitchen

THE UNIQUE FUNCTION OF THE PRESSURE COOKER

Each piece of kitchen equipment has its own particular role to play in the running of the home and a pressure cooker (or pan) can be one of the most valuable. Its speciality is *speed* and whenever time is at a premium it is there to perform its unique function.

A LONG HISTORY

Pressure-cooking is not a new idea. The first cooker was made by a French engineer, Denis Papin, in the seventeenth century and was known as Papin's Digester. It was a large round cast-iron vessel with heavy clamps and a formidable pressure gauge on the lid. In 1682, at a dinner given by the Royal Society in London, the Digester was demonstrated and one of the guests recorded in his diary that 'all the food, both fish and flesh was cooked in a Digester with less than eight ounces of coal'. Following this initial success, other demonstrations were given at other functions and soon the vessel was put into commercial production. In this same form and with very little alteration, it was made and used right up to the early part of this century. But it was far too clumsy and complicated for use in today's kitchens. In the early 1930s a much simpler and lighter vessel was produced in America and this is the aluminium pressure cooker that we use today.

HOW THE PRESSURE COOKER WORKS

By 'pressure-cooking', we mean that foods are cooked in steam which, under a certain amount of pressure, comes up to a temperature much higher than the usual boiling or simmering point, and therefore cooks in a much shorter time than by ordinary methods. At a pressure of 15 lb or about 7·5 kg, the temperature is approximately

250 °F or 103·3 °C. This pressure is called 'High', or just 'cooking pressure'.

Building up the pressure is a quick and simple process. When the liquid in the pan has begun to boil and send off steam, the vent is closed (usually with a weight) and this prevents the steam from escaping in the usual way. The result is that inside the pan it builds up gradually to 5 lb (Low), 10 lb (Medium) and then 15 lb (High) with a corresponding rise in temperature. By lowering the heat under the pan, the pressure and temperature may be kept constant.

Never pressure-cook with fat only. No steam will form and the food will burn.

IS IT SAFE?

Every pressure cooker made by a reputable firm has on the lid a reliable safety valve. This is a small rubber disc let into the lid, making that place much weaker than the stout aluminium casting of the cooker itself. Should it be incredibly foolishly used and all the rules and instructions ignored, the safety valve would come into operation and release the steam inside. This would reduce the pressure and temperature in a matter of seconds.

Betty MacDonald in her book *The Egg and I* described an incident in which her pressure cooker blew up. Now this was either put in to enhance a good story or the cooker was both faulty and flimsy. No pressure cooker made with thick strong aluminium and with a safety valve could possibly blow up. I have used a pressure cooker since 1946 and nothing of the sort has ever happened to me. Nor has it happened to any of the hundreds of people I have met who pressure-cook constantly.

To prove further the safety of the cooker, the Institute for the Blind have accepted pressure-cooking as safe for their people and have had the instructions and recipes issued in Braille.

BUYING A PRESSURE COOKER

Before setting out to make your purchase, make a firm decision about the size of pan that will be ideal for daily use for yourself and/or family. For four to six people the 7½–8 pint (4–4½ litre) size will be sufficient for all needs at all times. For seven or more a pan no larger than 11 pints (6 litres approx) will be more than adequate. But remember that this is a heavy pan in itself and with food for a large number added, the weight could deter you from pressure-cooking daily.

Turn a deaf ear to the salesman who tells you that in a large-sized pressure pan you can cook a *big piece of ham or other meat.* Pieces over 3 lb do not pressure-cook well. They become overcooked on the outside before the inside is tender. The 7½–8 pint (4–4½ litre) size will take a 3 lb (1½ kg) piece of meat and produce a delicious and perfectly-cooked pot roast in half the normal time. Because poultry is hollow inside, larger weights are possible. It is the solid piece that must not be over the 3 lb (1½ kg).

The saucepan type: This is the pan with the flat lid and the long handle and the most convenient size is the 7½–8 pint (4–4½ litre). I personally consider this the most useful and easy to handle of the three types of pressure pan, and it is the one I always use.

The casserole type: This may also be bought in the 4–4½ litre size. It has the advantage of lightness in weight and also of easy use and storage in the restricted space of a caravan or boat. It has some disadvantages and these should be mentioned. The turned-in sides makes pouring difficult and the two small handles are not as convenient as the long one customary in a saucepan. There is no definite way of judging the exact pressure during cooking, but a slight escape of steam quietly whispering will ensure that the pressure is being maintained.

The high dome type: This was designed with a 3 in high lid to enable enough food for about 16 people to be produced. But the weight of all that food, plus the weight of the pan and the heavy lid, would be too much for many people to carry. It has one special advantage in that it will take the taller quart-sized (1 litre) jars for preserving. But one must decide if it is worth carrying that weight around all the year just for a few weeks preserving in the summer. Today many people prefer to preserve in the smaller 1 pint (½ litre) jars and these may be accommodated in the smaller pan with the flat lid.

For the recipes in this book any pan of any size or shape may be used.

A MONEY SAVER

Only *low heat* on gas burners or electric coils is needed to maintain the pressure and this with the short cooking time *as well*, will result in a saving of money.

Most foods cooked under pressure will take about one-quarter of the time needed in an ordinary saucepan or casserole. But there are variations. For instance a whole piece of meat such as a pot-roast or cut of ham will need comparatively longer, about half the usual time. Very small things, such as split peas for soup, will take about one-eighth of the time. It is a case of the smaller the quicker, and the cheaper.

Some people may have been led to believe that one of the main functions of the pressure pan is to cook vegetables, but unless they are root vegetables needing 15 minutes or more in an ordinary saucepan, very little money is saved. The real economies are in cooking foods such as stews, casseroles and some soups, when from 1 to 2 hours may be saved.

TENDERISING TOUGH MEATS AND POULTRY

The pressure pan works wonders with shin meat and other tough meats and poultry. Instead of the long hours needed in an ordinary saucepan or casserole, it will produce a dish of tender meat, succulently flavoured and ready to serve, in a quarter of the time.

AFTER-OFFICE COOKING

If a repertoire of grills, fried foods and frozen-dinners has become threadbare from constant use, buy a pressure cooker. With it your range may be extended almost without limit to include casserole-style dishes of steak, chops and poultry, quick fish dishes, home-made soups with flavours you would never find in a packet or can, 5-minute custards, fruits, vegetables and a range of puddings and sweet dishes. All may be cooked and served after one gets home from work without delaying meal times.

BOAT, CARAVAN AND CAMPING

The pressure pan has proved to be so useful for holiday makers in yachts, caravans and tents that for many people it has become an accepted part of their equipment. Its speedy cooking means that if one is away on a day's sightseeing spree, there is no need to hurry back early to get a meal on the table. What a joy to be able to stay out as late as one dares, knowing that there will be no disapproving looks from hungry eyes!

BED-SIT MEALS ON ONE BURNER

If you have one burner that is your own absolutely, instead of being shared with four others, buy yourself a pressure pan, preferably the saucepan type. Choose the smallest on sale, 2 quart if possible; certainly not more than 7½ pint. With it you could cook any recipe in this book and many all-in-together meals. A few are suggested in the recipes, but you could invent many more. Remember that potatoes, onions and carrots can be cooked with any recipe needing not more than 20 minutes (*see p. 154*).

FAMILY MEALS

The pressure pan may not be needed for every family meal but there is usually some part for which its services would be invaluable. For instance, the soup for one meal, potatoes for another, the main course for another, and so on. This is better than struggling to find a whole meal that may be cooked at the same time. Few foods take exactly the same time to cook and it is a nuisance to have to open up the pan and go through all the processes again to put in quicker-cooking foods.

On the other hand, there are also ways of using the pan for more than one part of a meal. A pudding or other dessert could be cooked earlier in the day, leaving the pan free for either soup, vegetables or the main course; or, in the case of *Pot au Feu* (*p. 50*), all three together. Just let the pressure pan be your servant and serve you when you need it.

2. General Directions for Pressure-Cooking

HOW TO USE YOUR PRESSURE COOKER

1. Unless a recipe says 'insert rack or trivet', always remove it before starting to cook. When all the ingredients for the recipe have been placed in the pressure cooker, put on the lid (described as 'Fix the lid' throughout the recipes). It is very important to make sure that the lid is correctly adjusted according to the make of your cooker.
2. Where food is cooked on a rack or trivet, this can easily be lifted out by using a fairly long-handled pointed spoon, simply by inserting the point of the spoon into one of the slits. Still held by the point of the spoon, the rack can then be gently shaken to remove any sauce which may be adhering to it.
3. When plain water is heated in an aluminium vessel the oxygen causes discoloration. This is not dangerous to health, but spoils the look of the inside of your pan: it happens when food is cooked in a bowl, with only water in the pan. To counteract it, *add a little acid.* This could be 1 tablespoon of vinegar or lemon juice, or a piece of lemon rind. When you are using a lemon in a recipe, save the rind and put it into the refrigerator. Put it in the water in the pressure pan when making anything in a bowl. Another idea is to put 2 level teaspoons of cream of tartar in a jug with 1 pint (500 ml) of water. When needed, use 2 tablespoons in 1½ pints (750 ml) of water in the pressure pan.
4. Turn the heat full on under the pan: again consult the booklet. Some makers will tell you to wait until the steam is pouring from the vent before it is closed with the weight. Others will allow you to close it immediately without waiting for the flow of steam.
5. When the weight is on (the vent thus closed), continue heating

until the desired pressure is reached. This is almost invariably 15 lb or High. A few recipes in this book specify 10 lb pressure or Medium, and 5 lb pressure or Low. *Where the pressure is to be 15 lb only the words 'bring to pressure' are used.*

6. Now lower the heat. Only a small amount of gas or electricity will be needed to keep the pressure constant.
7. Time the cooking from this moment. A timer is a help to the memory (if you can remember to set the timer!).
8. When the cooking time is up, remove the pressure pan from heat. In the great majority of recipes, pressure is reduced at once. This may be done in two ways:
   (i) Have ready a basin of cold water and put the cooker into it (it needs only 1½ in of water).
   (ii) This is the most usual: lift the cooker over to the sink and turn the cold tap on to the side or the lid. Do not pour over the weight. As soon as cold water touches even a small part of the cooker, the pressure inside rapidly decreases to normal. Where the recipe says 'reduce pressure gradually', move the pan to a cool surface (the work top nearest to the gas or electric cooker) and leave it until the pressure has slowly reduced to normal. This will take from 3–5 minutes, depending upon the amount of food inside.
9. When pressure is normal, lift off the weight and remove the lid. (Always put the weight in the same place. Then you can reach for it quickly when you need it.) Wash the lid at once by running water through the vent. This will ensure that it is clean and ready for the next time.
10. Store the pan with the lid *upside-down* on top.
11. *When you have bought the pan, use it as much as possible.* This way the process will soon seem simple and all these rules will become second nature.

Note: Try not to drop the weight. The mechanism could be put out of line.

QUICK SUMMARY OF DIRECTIONS

1. Follow recipe and when all ingredients are in the pan, fix the lid.

2. Put on the weight, either before the steam is pouring out, or afterwards, depending on the make of pan.
3. Bring to pressure 15 lb, or High, unless otherwise indicated.
4. Take the time from the moment the pressure has been reached.
5. When time is up, remove pan from heat and reduce pressure.
6. Lift off weight and remove lid.

RULES FOR SAFETY

1. Make sure that there is at least ¼ pint (125 ml) water in the pressure pan before you begin. This is sufficient for foods needing up to 10 minutes pressure-cooking. Foods needing from 10 to 20 minutes need ½ pint liquid, although more could be added if you like plenty of gravy. In the recipes needing more than 20 minutes, correct amounts of liquid are given in the recipes.
2. See that the vent is clean before you begin. A rinse under the tap after use will clear it and leave it ready for the next time.
3. Do not fill the pressure pan more than two-thirds of its capacity with gravy or other liquid. For soups, or stewed apple which froths up, fill half full. Solids such as potatoes or other root vegetables placed on top of casserole dishes may occupy three-quarters of the pan's capacity (*see p. 24*).
4. Do not go away while the heat under the cooker is full on and the steam is building up. Stay near and regulate the heat when the 15 lb pressure is reached. A timer is invaluable. Set it the moment the pressure has reached the 15 lb and time the cooking from then. The instructions with your own make of cooker will disclose their method of indicating when the right pressure has been reached.
5. Do not try to lift off the weight before the pressure has returned to normal. Wait until it has given its final hiss and sigh, then lift it off with a cloth (because it is hot!) and put it in its usual place.

ELECTRICITY, GAS OR HEAT-STORAGE COOKERS

Electricity: Now that the old slow-heating-and-cooling electric elements have been replaced by the coil type and the quick-disc, the heat under the pressure pan can be regulated far more easily. All the same, even these new elements will still hold the heat a little longer than the gas jet. With the coil and quick-disc elements, keep the heat full on under the pan until a pressure of 10 lb or Medium has been reached, then turn down to 1 and the remaining heat will suffice to bring the pan to High. Use only sufficient heat (this is very little) to keep the pressure constant.

Gas: Have the heat full on under the pan until the required pressure has been reached then turn down very low. Only a bead of gas will be needed to keep the pressure constant. If you find that with natural gas it is difficult to prevent the pressure building up too much, move the pan to the side and subject it to only half the jet.

Heat-storage cookers: (These once used solid fuel only, but are now adapted to oil or gas.) For pressure-cooking, these stalwarts are just as convenient as gas or electric cookers. The pressure may be built up on the boiling-hob-plate and kept constant on the simmering one. If the heat is too great in the centre, move the pan towards the edge.

THE PRESSURE COOKER AS AN ORDINARY SAUCEPAN

By using an enamel plate instead of the cooker-lid, the pan may be used as an ordinary saucepan and this can save the expense of buying a separate large-sized saucepan. You then have the double advantage of having a pressure cooker which is also a heavy-based saucepan.

ALTITUDE PRESSURE-COOKING

Not many people will need to cook at high altitudes but it is worth noting that when a pressure pan is used in an aeroplane galley or by mountaineers at high altitudes, extra time is needed to bring the pressure to 15 lb and about 10 per cent more time for cooking.

THE PRESSURE COOKER AND THE FREEZER

Cooked foods: When taken from the deep freeze these may be thawed swiftly in the pressure pan. Pour in ¼ pint (125 ml) water, insert rack or trivet and put in the frozen food. Bring to pressure, then immediately move the pan to a cool surface and let the pressure reduce gradually.

Uncooked meats and poultry: These should thaw out *completely* before pressure-cooking.

Frozen green vegetables such as peas and beans could be pressure-cooked without thawing, but as they would take only one minute and could easily become overcooked it is not worth the trouble. It is simplest and best to cook them in an ordinary saucepan.

3. Using the Recipes

POINTS TO NOTE

Timing: All have been triple-tested and the pressure-cooking times checked for accuracy. In each case I have tried to make certain that when the time is up and the pan is opened, the food will be cooked to perfection, for I know how annoying it is to find that it is under-cooked. Not only does it mean that the meal has to be postponed, but also the process of bringing up the pressure, timing it, and reducing it again has to be repeated.

Food pressure-cooked in a metal or plastic container needs 2 minutes less than that cooked in other types of heat-proof containers. When using recipes where a metal or plastic container is suggested, remember to allow the extra 2 minutes if you use a utensil made of some other substance.

There may be instances when you need to make a few adjustments for yourself. For instance, if the meat you are using is tenderer and of a better quality than that given in the recipe, times could be reduced by 5 to 10 minutes. But as a rule, the more expensive cuts are kept for grilling and roasting. As I have explained, cooking times depend on toughness and size. As with ordinary heat, the high pressure-raised heat takes longer to penetrate into the centre of larger pieces of meat or other foods than into smaller ones.

Flavour and seasoning: Because all air is excluded and very little steam escapes, the flavour of pressure-cooked food is held in and cannot escape. All that is needed to bring out the combination of flavours you have chosen is the correct amount of salt and pepper. Very little liquid evaporates while pressure-cooking, which means that you will have more gravy or broth than in an open pan or casserole. For this reason, more salt and pepper will be needed for pressure-cooked food. In any flavouring, plain or pressure-cooked, you should just be able to taste the salt. Add no more after that.

There is always the perfect meeting place between food and salt and food and sugar. For instance apple, lemon or any other acid fruits will combine with sugar at an optimum point and the clever cook will know just where that is. In lemon curd, the flavour of lemon is at its most glorious: the rendezvous is perfect.

Herbs: Quantities indicated are for dried herbs as for most people, especially in the winter months, these are most readily available. Where fresh herbs are being used, double the quantity suggested.

Removing fat: In many instances it is advisable to remove as much fat as possible from the liquid in which meat or poultry has been cooked. In some cases one can pour the liquid into a basin and allow it to cool before removing the fat from the surface, but a quick method is to pour the liquid into a tall, slender jug in which the fat will fairly quickly rise to the surface, enabling it to be removed with little delay.

Thickening: The gravies and soups have in the majority of cases been thickened slightly before pressure-cooking. This not only saves the time and bother of last-minute thickening, but also means that the flour is thoroughly cooked.

Foil: When covering containers with foil, make quite sure that it has no holes or little tears in it.

Reducing pressure: It is important that instructions in some recipes to reduce pressure gradually are followed (*see p. 18*).

ADAPTING YOUR OWN RECIPES TO THE PRESSURE COOKER

The most valuable part of a book on pressure-cooking is the advice on timing. If the author fails to give correct timing, the book might as well go out of the window. True, the recipes may be useful and many people will persevere and find out their own times; others won't bother and will blame the pressure cooker. Once you have mastered the art of timing, you will be able to adapt any recipe to the pressure pan, provided it is a dish with gravy or liquid of some sort.

Adding whole potatoes and other vegetables: When putting vegetables on top of stews or other such dishes, the pressure pan may be filled to three-quarters capacity. So long as there remains about 1 in at the top for the circulation of steam, no harm can result. It is the gravy or other liquid that must not fill the pan more than two-thirds.

MEASUREMENTS

In former days when British cooking was at its best, measurements were surprisingly haphazard. Quantities were given in cups, spoons and handfuls and the liquid had to be sufficient for a 'good consistency'. Today chefs still throw a pile of flour on the marble slab when about to make pastry and pick up a bottle of wine and *pour* when making some delicious dish.

The metric equivalents given in recipes cannot be exact; they are approximate but always proportionate. *It is, therefore, important to stick to imperial or metric measurements within each recipe and not switch from one to the other.*

As cooking is not an *exact* science the metric measures have been rounded off in order to ease the transition in the kitchen. The following table is used here.

Weight

Kilogram is shown as kg. It is a little over 2 lb.
Gram is shown as g. This is a very tiny amount.
25 g may replace 1 oz.
100 g may replace 4 oz.
500 g may replace 1 lb which may be called ½ kg.

Liquids

Litre is shown as l and is a little over 1¾ pints.
Millilitre is shown as ml and is one-thousandth of a litre.
125 ml may replace ¼ pint or 1 gill.
250 ml or ¼ l may replace ½ pint.
500 ml or ½ l may replace 1 pint.

Do not feel that the cooking has to stop when faced with measurements in the metric system. If you wished you could ignore it and return to the quick and simple methods of our ancestors. All you need is a cup that will hold ½ pint of liquid and a set of measuring spoons. Here is a general table:

1 cup of liquid	½ pint or 10 fluid oz or ¼ litre	approx.
1 cup of flour	5½ oz or 138 g	,,
1 cup of granulated sugar	8 oz or 200 g	,,
1 cup of icing sugar	6 oz or 150 g	,,
1 cup of rice	8 oz or 200 g	,,
1 cup of sultanas	4 oz or 100 g	,,
1 cup of breadcrumbs	2 oz or 50 g	,,
1 level tablespoon butter	½ oz or 12·5 g	,,
1 rounded tablespoon butter	1 oz or 25 g	,,
1 rounded tablespoon sugar	1 oz or 25 g	,,
2½ level tablespoons flour	1 oz or 25 g	,,

Note: If you haven't a ½ pint cup, use your measuring jug instead. It will have the usual ¼, ½ and 1 pint lines and these could be also used for measuring solids. For instance, 5½ oz of flour will come up to the ½ pint line and so will 8 oz of sugar and rice. Your measuring spoons will deal with the odd measurements such as 3 oz etc. Follow the table set out above.

American measurements

1 cup	8 fl oz liquid	All measurements level
1 cup	4½ oz flour or cornflour	
1 cup	7 oz rice	

1 tablespoon	½ oz flour	All measurements level
1 tablespoon	¾ oz sugar	
1 tablespoon	¾ oz butter	

RECIPES

1. Soups

For flavour, nourishment and food-bill-economy, pressure-cooked soups are unbeatable and cost only about a quarter of the price of canned and packet soups. Enough for 6–8 servings may be made in the pressure pan.

Each soup contains health-giving ingredients and many are sturdy enough to be used for the main course for lunch or supper. Some are derived from old traditional recipes, others are specifically for vegetarians and a number are elegant enough for party occasions.

Soups that need hours of cooking in an ordinary saucepan take only a few minutes in the pressure pan. Pea Soup, for instance (a valuable source of protein), will cook to perfection, without any initial soaking of the peas, in 22 minutes instead of the usual 2 hours; Lentil Soup in 12 minutes, French Onion Soup in 8 minutes, and so on.

In this chapter there are recipes for a wide variety of delicious soups. Use the recipes as a guide should you wish to pressure-cook soups from your other cookbooks, or to invent some of your own.

Some recipes call for stock and instructions for making this are on *pp. 53 and 54.*

ALMOND SOUP (ancient and modern)

Time: 8 minutes *Serves 6*

An Almond Soup was made back in the fifteenth century, but to try and use the old 'receipt' today would be a tall order. Here it is:

> 'Pound some almonds and mix with beef broth and put it in a pot with cloves, maces, figs, currants and minced ginger and let all this seethe. Take bread and steep it in sweet wine and add to almonds. Add some sugar, then some rabbits or squirrels and partridges parboiled. *For a Lord* fry them whole. Otherwise chop into goblets and cast them into the pot and let them all boil to-

gether. Colour with sandlewood and saffron. Add vinegar and powdered cinnamon stained with wine and give it a boil . . .'

TWENTIETH-CENTURY VERSION

2 level tablespoons butter or margarine
1½ level tablespoons flour
2 onions, peeled and chopped finely
1½ pints (¾ litre) stock, or water with 2 chicken stock cubes
½ teaspoon almond essence
salt and pepper to taste
1 rounded teaspoon sugar
½ pint (¼ litre) milk
3 tablespoons cream
4 level tablespoons ground almonds
(The bowls may be topped with whipped cream laced with 2 tablespoons brandy and 1 teaspoon sugar)

1. Melt butter or margarine in pressure pan. When sizzling add the flour and cook without browning for 2 minutes. Remove from heat.
2. Add onions and stir, then add liquid, essence and seasoning. Mix well.
3. Fix lid and bring to pressure. *Allow 8 minutes.*
4. Reduce pressure and remove lid. Add milk, cream and ground almonds. Check for seasoning. Serve hot or chilled. The cream and brandy topping is a special treat.

ARTICHOKE (JERUSALEM) SOUP

Time: 10 minutes *Serves 6*

Jerusalem artichokes make a delicious and delicately flavoured soup which may be served hot or chilled.

1 lb (½ kg) Jerusalem artichokes
1 level tablespoon butter or margarine
1½ level tablespoons flour
2 medium-sized onions, peeled and chopped
1½ pints (¾ litre) water
2 chicken or veal stock cubes
1 bay leaf
3 sticks of celery, chopped, or other celery flavour (see step 3)
salt and pepper to taste
½ pint (¼ litre) milk
4 tablespoons cream (optional)
about 1 tablespoon chopped parsley

1. Peel or scrape the artichokes. Cut into pieces and drop into cold water to prevent discoloration.
2. Melt butter or margarine in pressure pan, then add the flour. Cook together for 2 minutes. Remove pan from heat.
3. Add onions, water, cubes, bay leaf, celery and seasoning. If fresh celery is not available use instead celery salt, celery soup cubes, or 1 tablespoon celery soup powder. Drain artichokes and add. Stir everything together.
4. Return pan to heat and fix lid. Bring to pressure and *allow 10 minutes.*
5. Reduce pressure and remove lid.
6. Tip through a colander into a large bowl and press vegetables through: if they are well mashed but have not all gone through, just add the remainder to the soup. (Or purée soup in Mouli or blender if preferred.)
7. Add milk and also the cream if liked. Reheat, adding the parsley.

To serve chilled: Add the cream and chill in the refrigerator until required. The bowls may be topped with whipped cream. Dust with a little paprika.

Artichoke soup with cheese: Top each bowl with about 1 tablespoon grated Cheddar or Parmesan cheese. (Only suitable for the hot soup.)

Artichoke soup with brandy: Add 3 or 4 tablespoons brandy to the hot or chilled soup, with 1 level teaspoon sugar.

ASPARAGUS CREAM SOUP (hot or chilled)

Time: 10 minutes *Serves 6*

If you grow your own asparagus, or buy it in large bundles, this recipe would take care of all those tough ends and turn them into an elegant soup for any occasion, winter or summer.

about 1 lb (½ kg) tough ends of asparagus spears (see above)
1 Spanish onion, peeled and chopped roughly
1 rounded tablespoon butter or margarine
3 level tablespoons flour
1½ pints (¾ litre) water

2 chicken stock cubes
1 level teaspoon sugar
salt and pepper to taste
½ pint (¼ litre) milk
4 tablespoons double cream or rich evaporated milk
about 1 tablespoon chopped parsley or chives

1. Wash and chop asparagus.
2. Melt butter or margarine in pressure pan. Add flour and cook together without browning for 1 minute. Remove from heat.
3. Add water, cubes, asparagus, onions, sugar and seasoning. Mix well and return to heat.
4. Fix lid and bring to pressure. *Allow 10 minutes.*
5. Reduce pressure and remove lid. Strain through a colander and press as much of the vegetable through as possible, discarding the remainder. (Or purée soup in Mouli or blender if preferred.)
6. Add milk and cream and reheat. Lastly add the parsley and/or chives. For a summer soup, chill in refrigerator and serve topped with whipped cream (laced with brandy for a special occasion).

BARLEY SOUP or SCOTCH BROTH

Time: 25 minutes *Serves 6–8*

Meg Dods, the Scottish cookery writer who published her book *The Cook and Housewife's Journal* in 1826, called this old traditional soup 'the bland, balsamic barley-broth of Scotland'. Her recipe is unchanged, but it is no longer the exclusive property of Scotland. It is made in every part of the British Isles, and was not left behind when the pioneers set off to find and settle the countries of the New World.

1–1½ lb (½–¾ kg) shin bone and its meat or neck of lamb
2½ pints (1¼ litres) water
4 tablespoons pearl barley
3 medium-sized onions, peeled and chopped
2 or 3 sliced carrots
2 turnips, diced
a few sticks of celery, if available, trimmed and cut into ½ in pieces
1 bay leaf
salt and pepper to taste
about ½ lb (¼ kg) green peas
chopped parsley (optional)

1. Put washed bones into pressure pan and add water and barley.
2. Prepare vegetables and add all but the peas. Add also the bay leaf and seasoning.

3. Fix lid and bring to pressure. *Allow 25 minutes.* The peas may be cooked meanwhile in an ordinary saucepan, or they may be added later and cooked without pressure.
4. Reduce pressure and remove lid. With a slotted spoon lift out the bones. The meat may be removed, cut up and returned to the soup.
5. Add the peas. If they are not already cooked, give them about 5 minutes in the soup. Check seasoning and serve piping hot. Parsley may be added to garnish.

BEEF CHOWDER

Time: 10 minutes *Serves 6*

A chowder is a soup in which the meat or fish and the vegetables are not strained out. The result is both appetising and satisfying.

½ lb (¼ kg) minced beef
1 level tablespoon flour
2 onions, any size, peeled and chopped
2 carrots and 2 parsnips, scraped and chopped or sliced
2 potatoes, any size, peeled and chopped or sliced
1½ pints (¾ litre) water
½ lb (¼ kg) tomatoes, skinned (or use canned)
½ teaspoon thyme
2 teaspoons sugar
salt and pepper to taste (2 teaspoons soy sauce may replace some of the salt)

1. Put beef and flour into pressure pan and cook together for 2 minutes. Remove from heat.
2. Add onions, carrots, parsnips, potatoes, water, tomatoes, thyme, sugar and seasoning. Mix well and return to heat. The soy sauce gives a delicious flavour.
3. Fix lid and bring to pressure. *Allow 10 minutes.*
4. Reduce pressure and remove lid. Check seasoning and serve without straining.

BEEF TEA or BROTH

Time: 10 minutes *Serves 4–5*

In the original edition of *Mrs. Beeton's Cookery Book* gratitude is expressed to the Americans for sending us their recipe for 'fluid beef'. She says, 'it is such a good substitute for alcoholic drinks in the cold weather, putting strength as well as life into our bodies when overcome by cold or fatigue.' This fascinating observation seems to have been eliminated from later editions.

1 lb (½ kg) lean stewing steak. Shin is ideal
1½ pints (¾ litre) cold water
1 onion, peeled and quartered
salt and pepper to taste
several sprigs of parsley

1. Trim the beef and cut it into ½ in pieces and drop into pressure pan. Add water, onion, seasoning and parsley. Allow to soak for ½ hour.
2. Fix lid and bring slowly to the boil on a low heat until steam is pouring from vent. Close vent and bring to pressure in the usual way. *Allow 10 minutes.*
3. Move pan to a cool surface and let the pressure reduce gradually.
4. Remove weight and lid. Strain the liquid and skim off fat if necessary before serving.

BORSCHT, or RUSSIAN BEETROOT SOUP

Time: 8 minutes *Serves 5–6*

There are many different recipes for *Borscht*, all traditional to some region of Russia. The basic ingredients are beetroot, stock, vegetables and a final addition of soured cream, though the latter may be omitted.

3 medium-sized beetroot, cooked, peeled and finely chopped (p. 153)
2 medium-sized onions, peeled and chopped
4 oz (100 g) cabbage, finely shredded and chopped
1¾ pints (875 ml) stock, or water with 2 beef stock cubes
2 tablespoons vinegar (preferably wine vinegar)
1 level tablespoon sugar
½ teaspoon tarragon
salt and pepper to taste
1 or 2 crushed cloves of garlic (optional)
about 6 tablespoons soured cream (optional)

1. Put the beetroot into the pressure pan with the onions, cabbage,

liquid, vinegar, sugar, tarragon and seasonings, including garlic if liked.

2. Fix lid and bring to pressure. *Allow 8 minutes.*
3. Reduce pressure and remove lid. The soup is delicious served as it is, but to be true to tradition, the soured cream may be added.

BOUILLABAISSE—A FISH SOUP

Time: 10 minutes *Serves 6–8*

The word '*bouillabaisse*' means boiling down to a mish-mash, so what better mish-masher could you have than your pressure pan? This is a famous Provençal soup, so when your travels take you to the sunny Mediterranean, try their *Bouillabaisse* and compare it with your own.

3 tablespoons olive oil
2 large leeks, washed and cut into ½ in pieces
1 large Spanish onion, peeled and chopped
2 rounded teaspoons flour
1½ pints (¾ litre) water
1½ lb (¾ kg) any boned and filleted fish of your choice, using one or more varieties
2 large potatoes, peeled and cut into ¼ in slices
1 or 2 crushed cloves of garlic
¼ teaspoon powdered saffron
½ lb (¼ kg) peeled tomatoes or a can
1 teaspoon mixed herbs
salt and pepper to taste and 2 teaspoons sugar
¼ lb (100 g) each of cooked shrimps and flaked lobster or crabmeat

1. Heat the oil in the pressure pan, then add the leeks, onion and flour. Cook together for 2 minutes. Remove from heat.
2. Add water, roughly-chopped fish (bones removed), then all the other ingredients except the shrimps and lobster or crabmeat. Season well with salt and pepper. Return to heat.
3. Fix lid and bring to pressure. *Allow 10 minutes.*
4. Reduce pressure and remove lid. Add the shrimps and lobster or crabmeat. Serve piping hot without straining.

CARROT SOUP WITH RICE

Time: 6 minutes *Serves 6–8*

A golden soup full of the special flavour of fresh carrots.

½ lb (200 g) carrots, scraped and grated coarsely
2 onions, peeled and chopped, or 2 large leeks, washed and cut into ¼ in slices, or both
2½ pints (1¼ litres) stock, or water with 3 chicken stock cubes
3 level tablespoons uncooked rice
1 bay leaf
salt and pepper to taste
1 tablespoon chopped parsley

1. Put the carrots, onions or leeks (or both) into the pressure pan.
2. Add all the other ingredients except the parsley.
3. Fix lid and bring to pressure. *Allow 6 minutes.*
4. Reduce pressure and remove lid. Check seasoning and add the parsley.

Note: 2–3 teaspoons vegetable concentrate may replace the chicken cubes.

CAULIFLOWER SOUP, or VICTORIAN WHITE SOUP

Time: 10 minutes *Serves 6–7*

The name 'White Soup' was given to several varieties of Victorian soups. Ground rice was a favourite thickening agent.

½ lb (¼ kg) cauliflower, chopped
2 onions, any size, peeled and chopped
4–6 sticks of celery, trimmed and chopped
1 level tablespoon butter or margarine
3 level tablespoons ground rice or flour
1½ pints (¾ litre) stock, or water with 2 chicken stock cubes
1 bay leaf
salt and pepper to taste
¼ pint (125 ml) milk or cream, or half and half
1 tablespoon chopped parsley

1. Melt the fat in pressure pan and add the vegetables. Cook for 2 minutes without browning. Stir in the rice or flour and cook for another minute. Remove from heat.
2. Add liquid, bay leaf and seasoning. Stir together and return to heat. Fix lid and bring to pressure. *Allow 10 minutes.*
3. Reduce pressure and remove lid. Either leave the soup as it is or

press through a colander into a large bowl or purée in Mouli or blender. Add the milk or cream and the parsley. Reheat, adding more seasoning if necessary.

Vegetarian cauliflower soup: Replace chicken stock cubes with 2–3 teaspoons vegetable concentrate.
Cauliflower soup with potatoes: Add to the vegetables 2 medium-sized peeled and chopped potatoes, preferably old ones.

CELERY SOUP, CHINESE STYLE

Time: 10 minutes *Serves 5–6*

Since most cookbooks give recipes for celery soup, it seemed to be a good idea to find something new for a change. Here is an unusual assembly of ingredients, all combining to make an elegant party soup.

2 tablespoons dried shrimps
6 dried mushrooms, cut small
4 sticks of celery, trimmed and chopped into ½ in pieces
1¾ pints (875 ml) stock, or water with 2 chicken stock cubes
2 level tablespoons uncooked rice
2 teaspoons soy sauce
salt and pepper to taste
⅛ teaspoon monosodium glutamate (Accent)
4 tablespoons sherry

1. Soak shrimps and mushrooms for about 4 hours or overnight in ¼ pint (125 ml) water.
2. Place in pressure pan. Add the celery, stock, soy sauce, rice and seasoning, including the Accent.
3. Fix lid and bring to pressure. *Allow 10 minutes.*
4. Reduce pressure and remove lid. Add sherry and check seasoning. Serve hot without straining.

CHESTNUT AND CARROT SOUP

Time: 8 minutes *Serves 6–8*

An old-fashioned recipe that you might like to try when chestnuts abound. For a vegetarian soup, omit the bacon.

½ lb (¼ kg) chestnuts
2 rashers of streaky bacon, or for the vegetarian soup, 1 tablespoon butter or margarine
2 medium-sized onions, peeled and chopped
1 level tablespoon flour
2 pints (1 litre) water
2 carrots, any size, cleaned and sliced
½ teaspoon thyme or other herb
salt and pepper to taste
cream or milk (optional)
chopped parsley

1. To peel the chestnuts, make a slit with a sharp pointed knife on each narrow side and place in pressure pan. Add ½ pint (¼ litre) water. Fix lid and bring to pressure. *Allow 5 minutes.* Drain and tip on to a plate. Take off both outer and inner skins.
2. Remove rinds from bacon. Cut into ½ in pieces and drop into pressure pan. Add onions and fry with the bacon for 3 minutes. Add flour and fry for another minute. Remove from heat. (For vegetarian soup, use the butter or margarine instead.)
3. Add water, carrots, chestnuts, herb and seasoning. Mix well and return to heat.
4. Fix lid and bring to pressure. *Allow 8 minutes.*
5. Reduce pressure and remove lid. Press everything through colander into a large bowl to make a creamy soup, or purée in Mouli or blender. Add cream or milk if liked, then sprinkle each bowl with chopped parsley.

CHICKEN SOUP (BELGIAN STYLE)—LE WATERZOÏE

Times: 20 minutes for chicken
40 minutes for boiling fowl
Serves 6

The broth is made while a boiling fowl or chicken is cooking. Afterwards the broth may be served as it is or used as a basis for any chicken soup. The bird is eaten with a sauce as a main course.

1 prepared chicken or boiling fowl, about 3–3½ lb (1½–1¾ kg), with giblets
2 pints (1 litre) water
2 whole onions, each stuck with 2 cloves
6 sticks of celery, trimmed and cut into ½ in pieces
2 carrots, cleaned and sliced
1 bay leaf
½ teaspoon thyme
plenty of salt and pepper

¼ pint (125 ml) white wine (optional)
a few chopped parsley stalks (the heads may be chopped and added afterwards)

1. Insert rack in pressure pan and put the bird on it. Pour in the water. Add onions, celery, carrots, herbs and seasoning. Fix lid and bring to pressure. *Allow times shown above.*
2. Meanwhile boil the giblets in ½ pint (¼ litre) water for 20 minutes.
3. Reduce pressure and remove lid. Lift out the bird.
4. Strain in the broth from the giblets, then add the wine (if liked) and the chopped parsley.
5. The broth may be strained and used as it is, or used as the basis for any chicken soup, thick or thin.
6. The bird may be served with a sauce (*see Chapter 7*) or be carved and served cold with a salad or used for a picnic. It will be deliciously flavoured.

CHICKEN LIVER AND NOODLE SOUP

Time: 6 minutes *Serves 4*

If you wish to serve 6–8 people, your 7½ or 8 pint pan will take twice the quantity given below. The recipe makes a nourishing soup, sturdy enough for the main course of a luncheon.

¼ lb (100 g) streaky bacon rashers
½ lb (¼ kg) chicken livers
1 medium-sized onion, peeled and finely chopped
1 level tablespoon flour
1½ pint (¾ litre) water (part red wine may be used)
¼ teaspoon thyme
1 beef stock cube
salt and pepper to taste (2 teaspoons soy sauce may replace some of the salt)
1 oz (25 g or ½ cup) egg noodles (see step 7)

1. Remove rinds from rashers and cut into ½ in pieces with scissors. Drop into pressure pan and begin to fry gently.
2. Trim and chop livers into tiny pieces.
3. Add onion and flour to bacon and fry together for 1 minute. Add chicken livers and cook for another minute.
4. Remove from heat and add liquid, thyme, stock cube and seasoning. Mix well and return to heat.
5. Fix lid and bring to pressure. *Allow 6 minutes.*

6. Reduce pressure and remove lid.
7. Add noodles and cook without pressure for 4 minutes, or until noodles have softened. For a sturdier soup, use 1½ oz or 2 oz noodles. Check seasoning before serving.

COCK-A-LEEKIE

Time: 40 minutes *Serves 6–8*

This traditional Scottish soup is often served as a starter for the annual Burns dinner, with haggis as the triumphal finish. The addition of prunes has not met with complete approval in Scotland and one forthright Scot is reported as saying 'speaking o' cock-a-leekie, the man who first polluted it with prunes was an atheist'!

1 boiling fowl, about 3–3½ lb (1½–1¾ kg)
2 pints (1 litre) water
1 whole peeled onion, stuck with 4 cloves
1 bay leaf
2 level tablespoons rice
1 lb (½ kg) leeks, trimmed and cut into ½ in rings
2 carrots, scraped and sliced
salt and pepper to taste
6 oz (150 g) cooked, stoned, chopped prunes

1. Truss the fowl and put into pressure pan. Add the water, onion, bay leaf and 2 teaspoons salt.
2. Fix lid and bring to pressure. *Allow 30 minutes.*
3. Reduce pressure and remove lid. Take out bay leaf.
4. Add rice, leeks, carrots, more salt and pepper to taste and the prunes. Fix lid again and bring to pressure. *Allow 10 minutes.*
5. Reduce pressure and remove lid. Lift out the bird. It may be served hot with a sauce (*see Chapter 7*) or cold with a salad. Serve the soup without straining.

COD AND SWEET CORN SOUP

Time: 6 minutes *Serves 6*

These two flavours seem born to harmonise. In a soup they combine to make an unusual first course or a nourishing meal for an invalid or convalescent. Remember it too when you are planning a winter dinner party.

½ lb (¼ kg) skinned boned cod
1 large Spanish onion, peeled and chopped
1 level tablespoon butter or margarine
1 level tablespoon flour
1 tablespoon anchovy sauce
1 pint (½ litre) water
salt and pepper to taste (fish should be salty)
1 bay leaf
1 or 2 bulbs of fennel, chopped (optional)
1 can cream-style sweet corn, about 8–10 oz (200–250 g)
½ pint (¼ litre) milk or half milk and half cream
chopped parsley (optional)

1. Wash cod and cut into ¾ in pieces.
2. Melt the butter in pressure pan. Add onion and cook 1 minute. Add flour and cook for another minute.
3. Add fish and mix in, then add the sauce, water, seasoning and bay leaf. Add also the fennel if liked. Mix well.
4. Fix lid and bring to pressure. *Allow 6 minutes.*
5. Reduce pressure and remove lid. Mash the fish. Remove bay leaf.
6. Add the sweet corn and the milk, or milk and cream. Taste and add more seasoning if necessary. Add parsley if liked and reheat before serving.

CUCUMBER CHILLED SOUP

Time: 10 minutes *Serves 6*

A summertime soup with a sophisticated air and a memorable flavour.

1½ level tablespoons butter
2 level tablespoons flour
about 1 lb (½ kg) cucumber, peeled and finely chopped
6 spring onions, chopped
½ teaspoon basil
1½ pints (¾ litre) water
salt and pepper to taste
1 small packet of frozen peas, or 1 cup fresh, shelled
1 teaspoon sugar
¼ pint (125 ml) cream
1 tablespoon chopped parsley

1. Melt butter in pressure pan and add flour. Cook together without browning for 2 minutes. Remove from heat.
2. Add cucumber, onions, basil, water, seasoning, peas and sugar. Mix well and return to heat.

3. Fix lid and bring to pressure. *Allow 10 minutes.*
4. Reduce pressure and remove lid. Tip into a colander over a large bowl and press the vegetables through or purée them in the blender or Mouli.
5. Add the cream and parsley. Chill. Serve in bowls topped with more chopped parsley, or chopped mint.

CUCUMBER AND SALMON SOUP (hot or chilled)

Time: 10 minutes *Serves 6*

Cucumber and salmon are two flavours that marry perfectly and good cooks bring them together for many different types of dishes. This soup is one of the best and is equally delicious whether served hot on a cold day or chilled on a warm one.

2 rounded teaspoons butter
1 large leek, washed and cut into ¼ in pieces
2 rounded teaspoons flour
about 8 oz (200 g) cucumber, peeled and finely chopped
1 8 oz (200 g) can of red salmon
1½ pints (¾ litre) water
1 rounded teaspoon sugar and salt and pepper to taste
1 tablespoon anchovy sauce
4 tablespoons double cream
1 tablespoon chopped parsley
whipped cream and brandy topping (optional)

1. Melt the butter in the pressure pan, then add the leek. Cook for 1 minute then add the flour and cook without browning for another 2 minutes.
2. Add the cucumber, mash the salmon (remove bits of skin and bone), then add it to the pan with its liquor, the water, sugar, seasoning and anchovy sauce. Stir all together.
3. Fix lid and bring to pressure. *Allow 10 minutes.*
4. Reduce pressure and remove lid. Add the cream and parsley. Serve either hot or chilled. The chilled soup may be topped with whipped cream laced with brandy.

FISH AND POTATO CHOWDER

Time: 15 minutes *Serves 8*

A thick nourishing soup, full of the goodness of fish, potatoes and leeks, and to heighten the overall flavour an extra and unexpected ingredient, the bacon rashers.

¼ lb (100 g) bacon rashers
1 lb (½ kg) fish fillets (any type such as cod, haddock, or a mixture)
1 lb (½ kg) potatoes, peeled
1 level tablespoon flour
about ½ lb (200 g) leeks, washed and trimmed
2½ pints (1¼ litres) water
1 bay leaf
1 clove of garlic, crushed (optional)
1 tablespoon lemon juice
salt and pepper to taste
¼ pint (125 ml) milk
¼ pint (125 ml) cream or evaporated milk
chopped parsley to garnish (optional)

1. Remove rinds from bacon and cut into ½ in pieces. Drop into pressure pan and begin to fry.
2. Skin fish and make sure there are no bones left. Cut into 2 in pieces.
3. Cut potatoes and leeks into ¼ in pieces.
4. When fat has run out from bacon add flour and cook for 1 minute. Add fish, potatoes and leeks, then water, bay leaf, garlic, lemon juice and seasoning. Stir well.
5. Fix lid and bring to pressure. *Allow 15 minutes.*
6. Reduce pressure and remove lid. Add milk and cream (or evaporated milk). Sprinkle with the parsley if liked. Reheat before serving.

FRENCH ONION SOUP

Time: 10 minutes *Serves 6*

Like Minestrone, this is another Continental soup that has come to stay. With its thick body of onions, and the toast and its sizzling cheese topping, it is frequently served as a main dish for lunch or supper.

1 level tablespoon butter or margarine
1 level tablespoon flour
1 lb (½ kg) onions, peeled and sliced
2 pints (1 litre) stock, or water with 2 chicken stock cubes
1 level teaspoon sugar
salt and pepper to taste (part celery salt may be used)
1 or 2 crushed cloves of garlic (optional)

slices of toast and grated Cheddar or Parmesan cheese
2 or more tablespoons brandy (optional)

1. Melt butter in pressure pan and add flour and onions. Cook for 2 minutes without browning.
2. Add liquid, sugar, seasoning and, if you like it, the garlic. Stir well.
3. Fix lid and bring to pressure. *Allow 10 minutes.*
4. Meanwhile make the toast, butter it and cover thickly with the grated cheese. Sprinkle with salt and pepper. Grill until cheese is sizzling and faintly browned.
5. Reduce pressure and remove lid. Add brandy if liked. Check seasoning.
6. Pour into heated bowls. Put a slice of cheesy toast on each and serve at once.

GIBLET SOUP WITH MUSHROOMS

Time: 10 minutes *Serves 3–4*

The quantity used in this recipe is for the one set of giblets usually found inside an oven-ready bird. To double the servings, either buy another set, or ½ lb of chicken livers, and double the other ingredients.

1 rasher of streaky bacon
1 rounded teaspoon butter or margarine
2 rounded teaspoons flour
1 large onion peeled and chopped
1 set chicken giblets
1½ pints (¾ litre) stock, or water with 1 beef stock cube
1 clove of garlic, crushed (optional)
1 teaspoon celery salt
salt and pepper to taste
4 oz (100 g) mushrooms, washed and sliced
2 or 3 tablespoons brandy (optional)
chopped parsley (optional)

1. Cut bacon into 2 in pieces. As the soup will be strained, the rinds will not need to be removed. Drop bacon into pressure pan and begin to fry. Add the butter.
2. Add the flour and fry for 1 minute, then add the onions and fry for another minute. Remove from heat.
3. Trim and chop the giblets and add, then add the stock, celery salt, garlic and seasoning.

4. Mix well then return to heat. Fix lid and bring to pressure. *Allow 10 minutes.*
5. Fry the mushrooms in a little butter.
6. Reduce pressure and remove lid. Strain into a bowl, then tip broth back into pressure pan. Add brandy if liked.
7. Lastly add the fried mushrooms. Chopped parsley may also be added.

LEEK AND POTATO SOUP (hot), VICHYSSOISE (chilled)

Time: 12 minutes *Serves 6–7*

For many generations in England this soup was eclipsed because of its dull and misleading name, 'Milk Soup'. I saw it in an old Family Receipt book and knew at once that it was really our popular Leek and Potato Soup and also (when served chilled) the famous Vichyssoise Soup of France.

1 lb (½ kg) leeks, washed and sliced
1 level tablespoon butter or margarine
2 rounded teaspoons flour
1 lb (½ kg) old potatoes, peeled and sliced or chopped
1 pint (½ litre) light stock or water with 2 chicken stock cubes
1 bay leaf
salt and pepper to taste
½ pint (¼ litre) milk, or half milk and half cream
1 tablespoon chopped parsley
2 or 3 sticks of celery, chopped (optional)

For VICHYSSOISE, see below

1. Melt the fat in the pressure pan and add leeks. Cook for 1 minute then add the flour and cook for another minute.
2. Add potatoes to pan, with the celery if liked. Add also the stock, bay leaf and seasoning.
3. Fix lid and bring to pressure. *Allow 12 minutes.*
4. Reduce pressure and remove lid. Either beat the potatoes to a mush in the soup, push through a colander.
5. Add the milk, or milk and cream and the parsley. More milk may be added. Check for seasoning.

Vichyssoise: Follow preceding recipe, using the cream. Sieve or liquidise the soup to make it smooth and creamy. Chill before serving. Sprinkle with more parsley, or finely chopped chives; top with a little whipped cream.

MINESTRONE

Time: 28 minutes *Serves 7–8*

Minestrone is a robust soup. It would be worth while to make a large bowl of it ready for when you or the family come home hungry and tired. A stand-by too for a quick one-course lunch. A lazier method is given in the next recipe.

4 oz (100 g) haricot beans
2½ pints (625 ml) water
2 rashers of streaky bacon
2 medium-sized onions, peeled and chopped
4 or more sticks of celery, trimmed and cut into ½ in pieces
½ lb (¼ kg) tomatoes, peeled and halved, or a can
salt and pepper to taste
3 oz (75 g) spaghetti, broken into 2 in pieces
1 tablespoon olive oil
2 teaspoons sugar
2 beef stock cubes
1 clove of garlic, crushed (optional)
1 small packet of frozen peas, or ½ lb (¼ kg) fresh

1. Soak the beans overnight, or for about 6 hours, in the water.
2. Tip beans and water into pressure pan. Fix lid and bring to pressure. *Allow 20 minutes.* Reduce pressure and remove lid.
3. Remove rinds from bacon and cut into ½ in pieces. Add to the beans with all the other ingredients except the peas.
4. Fix lid again and bring to pressure. *Allow 8 minutes.*
5. The peas may be cooked in a little salted water in a small saucepan, or they could be added after pressure-cooking.
6. Reduce pressure and remove lid. Add cooked peas and liquid, or cook them in the soup, without pressure, until tender.

MINESTRONE, QUICK METHOD

Time: 8 minutes *Serves 6*

A little cheating creates an equally robust and nourishing soup in a much shorter time and with much less trouble.

2 rashers of streaky bacon
1 teaspoon butter or oil
2 tablespoons dried onions
3 or 4 sticks of celery, trimmed and cut into ½ in pieces
2 pints (1 litre) water
2 teaspoons brown sugar
1 bay leaf
2 oz (50 g) macaroni or broken-up spaghetti
2 beef stock cubes
salt and pepper to taste
1 clove of garlic, crushed (optional)
1 small packet of frozen peas
a 1 lb (½ kg) can of baked beans in tomato sauce

1. Remove rinds from bacon and cut into ½ in pieces. Drop into pressure pan and begin to fry gently. Add the butter or oil.
2. Add onions and celery and fry with the bacon for 2 minutes.
3. Add the water, sugar, bay leaf, pasta, cubes, seasoning and garlic if used. Mix well. Fix lid and bring to pressure. *Allow 8 minutes.* Reduce pressure and remove lid. Take out bay leaf.
4. Tip in the frozen peas and cook without pressure for 4 minutes, then add the baked beans and cook for another 2 minutes. Check seasoning before serving.

MULLIGATAWNY SOUP

Time: 10 minutes *Serves 6–8*

This is the soup that was brought back to England by her Empire builders of the eighteenth and nineteenth centuries. It is excellent served either hot or chilled.

1½ level tablespoons butter
1 level tablespoon curry powder (or more if liked)
2 level tablespoons flour
2 pints (1 litre) stock or water with 2 beef stock cubes
1 bacon rasher, or a knuckle
2 onions, peeled and chopped
2 apples, peeled and sliced
1 bay leaf
1 level tablespoon brown sugar
plenty of salt and pepper
1 or 2 cloves of garlic, crushed (optional)

1. Melt butter in pressure pan, then stir in curry powder and flour. Cook together for 2 minutes, or until browned. Remove from heat.
2. Add stock, the bacon rasher or knuckle, the onions, apples, bay leaf, sugar and seasoning. Add garlic if liked.

3. Return to heat. Fix lid and bring to pressure. *Allow 10 minutes.*
4. Reduce pressure and remove lid. Take out bacon rasher or knuckle and the bay leaf. The rasher could be cut into small pieces and returned to the soup. Add more seasoning if necessary. Serve either hot or chilled.

MUSHROOM SOUP

Time: 3 or 8 minutes *Serves 4*

The timing varies according to the method of preparation. If you have an electric blender, the ingredients may be whizzed into tiny pieces, thus reducing pressure-cooking time to 3 minutes. Hand-chopped, they will need 8 minutes.

2 medium-sized onions, peeled and chopped
6 oz (150 g) mushrooms, preferably dark field ones, cleaned
1 crushed clove of garlic (optional)
2 rashers of streaky bacon
2 level tablespoons flour
1½ pints (¾ litre) water
2 beef stock cubes
½ teaspoon mixed herbs or thyme
a few dashes of monosodium glutinate (Accent)
salt and pepper to taste
sherry (optional)

1. If you have an electric blender, use it to whizz the onions, mushrooms and garlic into small pieces, adding ¼ pint (125 ml) of the water. Otherwise chop roughly by hand.
2. Remove rinds from rashers and cut into ½ in pieces. Drop into pressure pan and fry for 2 minutes.
3. Add flour and vegetables and toss around, cooking for another minute.
4. Add water, cubes, herbs, and Accent. Mix well, and add seasoning.
5. Fix lid and bring to pressure. *Allow 3 or 8 minutes* (see note above).
6. Reduce pressure and remove lid. Serve, well-seasoned, without straining. Add a little sherry if liked.

PEA-POD CREAM SOUP (hot or chilled)

Time: 15 minutes *Serves 6*

Vitamins and flavour are in those pea-pods that are usually thrown away but they can be used to make a delicious and appetising soup which may be served either hot or chilled.

pods from about 1–1½ lb (½–¾ kg) peas
½ lb (200 g) onions or leeks, chopped
spinach to give green colour (either 4/5 leaves, or a baby can of purée, or ½ small packet of frozen)
water (see step 1)
2 chicken stock cubes
salt and pepper to taste
½ pint (250 ml) Cream Sauce (p. 192)
1 teaspoon sugar
a little chopped mint
cream (optional) (see step 5)

1. Wash pods and place in pressure pan. Add onions or leeks and the spinach. Cover with enough water to fill the pan two-thirds.
2. Add the stock cubes and seasoning.
3. Fix lid and bring to pressure. *Allow 15 minutes.*
4. Reduce pressure and remove lid. Strain soup through a colander, pushing as much of the vegetable through as possible, or purée in Mouli or blender.
5. Tip soup back into the pan. Add the Cream Sauce, sugar and mint. If about 4 or more tablespoons of cream are added, especially if the soup is to be served chilled, it is doubly delicious.

PEA SOUP

Time: 22 minutes *Serves 6–8*

Split peas are stubborn little things and usually take from 2–2½ hours to soften. In the pressure pan they take only about one-eighth of the time, a saving well worth while.

6 oz (150 g or ¾ cup) split peas
2 pints (1 litre) water
1 small knuckle of ham or 1 bacon rasher, or a dozen or so bacon rinds
1 large onion, peeled and chopped
1 bay leaf or ½ teaspoon thyme
plenty of salt and pepper

1. Wash peas in a strainer and put into pressure pan. Add all the other ingredients. Stir together. Fix lid and bring to pressure. *Allow 22 minutes.*

2. Reduce pressure and remove lid. Take out knuckle or bacon (or rinds), and bay leaf if used. The soup will not require mashing as it will be sufficiently creamy.

Lentil soup: Use lentils instead of peas and *allow 12 minutes.*

POT-AU-FEU

Times: 50 minutes for 2 lb (1 kg) *Serves 6–7*
1¼ hours for 2½ lb (1¼ kg)
1½ hours for 3 lb (1½ kg)

This is the national family soup of France. It has its variations but basically it is a 'soup meal'. The broth is strained off first and served as a soup course and the meat and vegetables follow.

2–3 lb (1–1½ kg) topside or fresh brisket of beef in one piece, about 3 in thick
a little flour
2 tablespoons butter, oil or other fat
2 pints (1 litre) stock, or water with 1 beef stock cube
¼ pint red wine (125 ml) or ½ lb (¼ kg) peeled tomatoes (fresh or canned)
½ teaspoon mixed herbs
2 teaspoons brown sugar (if tomatoes are being used)
salt and pepper to taste
1 or 2 cloves of garlic, crushed (optional)
whole onions, carrots, parsnips and potatoes, all peeled (see step 5)

1. Trim the meat, rinse, then wipe dry with kitchen paper. Cover all over with flour.
2. Melt the fat in the pressure pan and brown the meat on all sides. Remove meat from pan. Tip away any surplus fat.
3. Insert rack and put meat back into pan. Add water, wine or tomatoes, herbs and seasoning, including garlic if liked.
4. Fix lid and bring to pressure. *Allow 15 minutes less than the times shown above.*
5. Reduce pressure and remove lid. Add the vegetables up to the two-thirds limit. Either add all the vegetables suggested, or choose just two or three.
6. Fix lid again and bring to pressure. *Allow the extra 15 minutes.* Reduce pressure and remove lid.

7. Strain out the broth and serve as the soup course, skimming off any surplus fat and adding more seasoning if necessary. Serve the meat and vegetables as the main course. Some of the remaining broth may be thickened and used for gravy.

QUEEN CAROLINE'S CONSOMMÉ

Time: 20 minutes *Serves 6*

This consommé, named after Caroline of Brunswick, George IV of England's Queen, has a base of beef broth, a substance of chicken and a garnish of Royal Custard.

about 1½ lb (¾ kg approx) meaty shin bone, fat removed
1 chicken leg
1 can jellied consommé made up to 2 pints (1 litre) with water
2 finely chopped onions
4 or 5 sticks of celery, cleaned and cut into ¼ in pieces
½ teaspoon mixed herbs
salt and pepper
brandy

ROYAL CUSTARD (see step 3):
1 large egg
2 tablespoons milk
a little salt and pepper
2 teaspoons butter

1. Put all ingredients (except those for Royal Custard, and the brandy) into pressure pan.
2. Fix lid and bring to pressure. *Allow 20 minutes.*
3. Meantime make Royal Custard. Beat the egg and milk and a little salt and pepper. Melt the butter in an 8 in frying-pan. Pour in the custard. Cover with an enamel plate and cook for about ½ minute or until set. Cool, then make criss-cross diagonal lines to cut custard into small diamonds.
4. Reduce pressure and remove lid. Strain broth into a bowl.
5. Lift out shin bone and remove marrow. Cut small and add to broth. Remove chicken from bones, chop finely and add this also to the broth.
6. Pour back into pressure pan or another saucepan. Reheat, check seasoning and add about 2 teaspoons brandy per serving, if liked. Serve garnished with the Royal Custard diamonds.

QUICK LENTIL AND TOMATO SOUP

Time: 12 minutes *Serves 5–6*

In this recipe the preparation is as speedy as the cooking. The lentils come from a packet, the tomatoes from a can and the potatoes and onions are dried. It is a thick nourishing soup for a chilly day.

4 oz (100 g) lentils
1¾ pints (875 ml) water
1 level tablespoon powdered dried potato, or 1 heaped tablespoon if in pieces
1 rounded tablespoon dried onions
about 8 oz (¼ kg) canned peeled tomatoes
1 chicken or veal stock cube
2 good teaspoons brown sugar
salt and pepper to taste
½ teaspoon sweet basil or herb of your choice

1. Put all ingredients into pressure pan.
2. Fix lid and bring to pressure. *Allow 12 minutes.*
3. Reduce pressure and remove lid.
4. Check seasoning. Serve without straining.

Note: Left-over bacon rinds or a rasher of bacon may be added. Remove before serving.

SCOTCH HOTCH-POTCH

Time: 20 minutes *Serves 8*

An old Scottish recipe, nourishing and sustaining. The lamb may be eaten separately, or slipped off the bones and added to the soup.

about 1 lb (½ kg) scrag end of neck of lamb
2½ pints (1¼ litres) water
2 rounded tablespoons barley
1 bay leaf
salt and pepper to taste
a hotch-potch of vegetables in any quantity and variety. They could be onions, carrots, leeks, celery, parsnips and potatoes, all chopped or sliced (see step 2)

1. Trim some of the fat from the lamb and put into pressure pan. Add the water, barley, bay leaf and seasoning.
2. Add any variety of vegetables but do not fill the pan more than two-thirds.

3. Fix lid and bring to pressure. *Allow 20 minutes.*
4. Reduce pressure and remove lid. Lift out the lamb and either remove bones and return meat to soup or serve separately. Skin off any surplus fat from soup, check seasoning, and serve piping hot.

A SPANISH SOUP WITH FISH

Time: 18 minutes *Serves 6–8*

A filling fish and dried pea soup that may be served as the main dish for a lunch, supper or high tea.

½ lb (¼ kg) lightly smoked fish
6 level tablespoons (4 oz or 100 g) dried split yellow peas
2 pints (1 litre) water
1 large Spanish onion, peeled and chopped
½ lb (¼ kg) peeled tomatoes (fresh or canned)
1 teaspoon sugar
1 teaspoon basil
salt and pepper to taste
1 crushed clove of garlic (optional)
1 small packet frozen peas or beans

1. Soak the fish in plenty of water for at least ½ hour to remove some of the salt.
2. Wash the dried peas in a fine strainer and put into pressure pan. Add the water, onion, tomatoes and sugar.
3. Take the fish from the water, skin, bone and flake it. Add to the other ingredients in the pressure pan. Add basil and seasoning—be careful not to add too much salt. The garlic may be added here. Stir everything together. Leave the peas or beans until later.
4. Fix lid and bring to pressure. *Allow 18 minutes.*
5. Reduce pressure and remove lid. Tip in the frozen peas or beans and cook for another 6 minutes or until done.

STOCK (LIGHT)

Time: 25 minutes *Makes 3 pints (1½ litres)*

The old-style kitchen range with its large area and constant heat could keep a stock pot at the side where it could simmer gently all day. Into it went bones, stalks and outer leaves of vegetables and anything that would give flavour and substance to a good stock. Today our modern cookers make this less practical, so instead we can either use canned bouillon, stock cubes, or resort to our pressure cooker.

a knuckle of veal, ham bone or a chicken carcase
2½ pints (1¼ litres) water
2 large whole onions, peeled
2 cloves
salt and pepper to taste
1 bay leaf
discarded parts of leeks, cauliflower stalks, outside leaves of cabbage, ends of celery or any other vegetables

1. Put all ingredients into pressure pan. Do not fill more than two-thirds.
2. Fix lid and bring to pressure. *Allow 25 minutes.*
3. Reduce pressure and remove lid. Lift out onions.
4. Strain into a large bowl. When cool put into refrigerator until needed. Remove surplus fat before using. The onions may be served as a vegetable.

STOCK (DARK)

This is made with beef bones. To darken it further, the onions could first be fried in a little oil or other fat until browned (but not burnt!), or a dark beef stock cube could be added.

TOMATO SOUP (FRESH)

Time: 6 minutes *Serves 6*

When tomatoes are cheap, or home-grown, a large pot of rich tomato soup may be made for half the price of the canned or packet varieties. In the 6 minutes cooking time the sago (don't use tapioca) will have dissolved away.

about 1½ lb (¾ kg) tomatoes quartered
1½ pints (¾ litre) water
1 rasher of bacon
2 peeled chopped onions
1 level tablespoon small sago
½ teaspoon basil or thyme
3 rounded teaspoons sugar
2 teaspoons Worcester sauce
salt and pepper to taste

1. As the soup will be strained, the tomatoes need not be peeled. Place them in the pressure pan with the rest of the ingredients.
2. Fix lid and bring to pressure. *Allow 6 minutes.*
3. Reduce pressure and remove lid. Strain through a colander into a large bowl. Push all the vegetables through, leaving behind the tomato skins. Remove the rasher, chop into very small pieces, and add to the strained soup. Check seasoning and reheat soup if necessary.

VEGETABLE SOUP

Time: 15 minutes *Serves 7–8*

Potatoes provide the body for this excellent soup. After cooking, all the vegetables may be either pushed through a colander, or whisked to a creamy consistency with an electric mixer.

1 level tablespoon butter or margarine
1 level tablespoon flour
2 onions, peeled and sliced
2 or 3 carrots, scraped and quartered
1 lb (½ kg) potatoes, peeled and sliced
about 2 cups of any other roughly chopped vegetables such as celery, leeks, tomatoes, parsnips, turnips, etc
2 pints (1 litre) water, or enough to fill the pan to two-thirds
1 bay leaf and some chopped parsley
salt and pepper to taste
1 rounded teaspoon sugar
2 teaspoons vegetable concentrate

1. Melt butter or margarine in pressure pan, then add flour. Cook together for 1 minute. Remove from heat.
2. Add onions, carrots, potatoes and other vegetables.
3. Add water, herbs, seasoning and vegetable concentrate. Mix well. Return to heat.
4. Fix lid and bring to pressure. *Allow 15 minutes.*
5. Reduce pressure and remove lid. Either push the vegetables through a colander or use an electric mixer. To do the latter, first strain off three-quarters of the broth, tip the rest into a mixer bowl and whisk until the vegetables are mushed to a creamy consistency. Add to the reserved broth. Heat the soup through and add more seasoning if necessary.

VEGETARIAN WHITE SOUP

Time: 6 minutes *Serves 6*

A wheat-free recipe, containing a vegetable concentrate and using either rice or small sago. (Don't use tapioca.) The sago dissolves away and secretly provides a little thickness.

2 medium-sized onions or leeks, or both, chopped
about 6 sticks of celery cut into ¼ in pieces, or a root of celeriac, washed and chopped small
4 potatoes or Jerusalem artichokes, peeled and sliced
2 parsnips, scraped and sliced
1½ pints (¾ litre) water
2 good teaspoons vegetable concentrate
2 level tablespoons uncooked rice or *1 level tablespoon small sago*
salt and pepper to taste
milk or cream (optional)

1. Tip vegetables into pressure pan. Add water, vegetable concentrate, rice or sago, bay leaf and seasoning.
2. Fix lid and bring to pressure. *Allow 6 minutes.*
3. Reduce pressure and remove lid. If liked, add a little milk or cream. Serve without straining.

WATERCRESS AND PUMPKIN CREAM SOUP (hot or chilled)

Time: 10 minutes *Serves 6–8*

A dry type of pumpkin will make the best soup. Using it as a basis, other ingredients such as carrots, cabbage or cauliflower may be used as well as or instead of the watercress.

1½ lb (¾ kg) pumpkin, peeled and cut into pieces
2 good handfuls of watercress, washed and chopped
additional vegetables (see above)
1 level tablespoon butter or *margarine*
2 level tablespoons flour
1½ pints (¾ litre) water
salt and pepper to taste
1 chicken stock cube
milk or cream
parsley, chopped

1. Melt the butter or margarine in pressure pan and add flour. Cook without browning for 2 minutes. Remove from heat.
2. Add water, pumpkin, cress, seasoning, cube and extra vegetables if used. Do not fill pan more than two-thirds.
3. Fix lid and bring to pressure. *Allow 10 minutes.*
4. Reduce pressure and remove lid. Push the soup through a colander into a large bowl or purée in Mouli or blender. Add milk or cream to taste and any amount of chopped parsley. Check seasoning. Reheat or serve chilled.

2. Fish Dishes and Dishes for Luncheon and Supper

This chapter contains a great variety of ideas for quickly made savoury dishes.

Some are arranged as all-in-together meals for those with only one burner or ring, others, such as Spaghetti-in-Tomato-Sauce will serve a hungry family.

The savoury custards (*p. 71 to p. 72*), are made in a quarter of the usual time and are useful for a great number of occasions. Note particularly the idea on *p. 74* for savoury darioles as a first course for a luncheon or dinner party. They won't spoil if left in the cooker after the pressure has reduced, but will keep hot for about 15–20 minutes.

FISH IN FOIL

Times: Fish $\frac{3}{4}$ in thick, 5 minutes
Fish 1 in thick, 7 minutes
Fish $1\frac{1}{2}$ in thick, 10 minutes

3 fish fillets or fish steaks
3 teaspoons butter
1 onion, peeled and grated
salt and pepper
1 bay leaf
3 dessertspoons wine or water, or part lemon juice and water

1. Have ready a piece of foil large enough to fold around each fillet or steak; place one on each piece.
2. Spread the fish with butter and a little grated onion, then sprinkle with salt and pepper. Break bay leaf into three pieces and place one on each fillet. Add 1 dessertspoon wine, water or lemon juice and water.
3. Fold the foil over and tuck in the ends to make parcels.

4. Pour ¼ pint (125 ml) water into pressure pan. Insert rack or trivet. Place parcels on rack. Fix lid and bring to pressure. *Allow times shown above.*
5. Reduce pressure and remove lid. Lift out parcels. Remove rack or trivet. A sauce could be made using the drippings and some of the liquid in the pressure pan (*see Chapter 7*).

FISH AND SAVOURY RICE ALL-IN-TOGETHER

Time: 6–8 minutes *Serves 2–3*

The savoury rice is cooked in the pressure pan and the fish in the dividers or a dish that will fit into the pan. Remember to allow an extra 2 minutes if a glass or china bowl is used. A useful recipe for one burner. The pressure pan will take double the quantity for more people.

1–1½ lb (½–¾ g) plaice or other thin fillets of fish
6 oz (150 g) long-grain rice
2 medium-sized tomatoes, skinned and sliced
1 pint (½ litre) water
2 teaspoons sugar
1 onion, finely chopped
2 teaspoons Worcester sauce
salt and pepper to taste
1 bay leaf (optional)
sauce (see chapter 7, *or use canned soup, any flavour)*

1. Put rice, tomatoes, water, sugar, onion and Worcester sauce into pressure pan. Add 1 level teaspoon salt and a little pepper.
2. Insert the rack or trivet.
3. Cut fillets into serving-sized pieces, and put into separators or a dish. Sprinkle with salt and pepper. A piece of bay leaf may be added to each fillet. Place on the rack or trivet.
4. Fix lid and bring to pressure. *Allow 5 minutes.*
5. Reduce pressure and remove lid. Lift out fish. Remove rack or trivet. Cook rice without pressure for about 3 more minutes to soak up liquid.
6. While dishing up, heat the sauce in a small saucepan. Any canned soup would make a quick tasty sauce—mushroom, celery, asparagus or vegetable.
7. Serve with sauce poured over fish. Sprigs of parsley would make an attractive garnish.

BED-SIT FISH DINNER

Time: 8 minutes *Serves 2–3*

Individual portions of fish are cooked in foil parcels, vegetables are cooked at the same time and a can of soup stands in for a tasty sauce. A salad would complete the meal.

1–1½ lb (½–¾ kg) fish fillets, any type
salt and pepper
a little lemon juice or wine
1 bay leaf, broken into small pieces
¼ pint (125 ml) water
½ teaspoon salt
potatoes for 2 or 3, peeled and cut into halves lengthwise
another vegetable such as whole carrots, whole small onions, or leeks cut into 2 in pieces, or a mixture
½ pint (250 ml) can of cream soup (any suitable flavour) heated
parsley, chopped

1. Have the fillets skinned by the fishmonger.
2. Cut squares of foil large enough to enclose a fillet in a parcel. Lay the fish on the foil, then sprinkle with salt, pepper and a little lemon juice or wine. Put a small piece of bay leaf on each. Fold the foil around and turn edges in.
3. Pour the ¼ pint water into the pressure pan, add the salt and potatoes. Place rack or trivet on top of the potatoes and place parcels on it. Arrange the other vegetables around and on top. Sprinkle with salt and pepper.
4. Fix lid and bring to pressure. *Allow 8 minutes.*
5. Reduce pressure and remove lid. Put soup for sauce in a small saucepan and heat while the dishing up is being done.
6. Lift out vegetables and parcels on rack; *see p. 17, para. 2.* Unwrap parcels and tip drippings into sauce. Strain liquid from potatoes and mash with a little milk and butter.
7. Serve with the sauce poured over the fish and a sprinkling of chopped parsley.

FISH STEAKS WITH CELERY-CHEESE SAUCE

Time: 7–10 minutes *Serves 4*

In this recipe the celery sauce is thickened with small sago instead of flour. It is a successful and lazy way and no one will guess. The sago dissolves away completely giving a smooth and perfect consistency.

fish steaks for 4 (cod, halibut, turbot or any other available fish)
1 level tablespoon butter or margarine
3 sticks of celery, trimmed and chopped into ½ in pieces
4 level teaspoons small sago (not *tapioca)*
¼ pint (125 ml) water
salt and pepper to taste
¼ pint (125 ml) milk or cream
3 oz (½ cup or 75 g) grated sharp cheese

1. Cut the skinned steaks into individual portion sizes.
2. Melt butter or margarine in pressure pan. Add celery, sago, water and seasoning.
3. Put rack into pan and lay the fish on it. Sprinkle with a little salt and pepper.
4. Fix lid and bring to pressure. *Allow 7 minutes* for steaks 1 in thick. If they are 1¼ in thick, allow 10 minutes.
5. Reduce pressure and remove lid. Lift rack out with pointed spoon, place fish on a dish and keep warm. Remove rack or trivet.
6. Add milk and cheese to celery sauce. Taste and add more seasoning if necessary. Serve with the fish.

SALMON MOULDS

Times: 8 minutes for individual moulds
15 minutes for 1 large mould *Serves 3*

An attractive idea for a television tray supper, or a luncheon threesome. The mixture is put into small ⅛ pint moulds, placed on the rack in the pressure pan and cooked for just 8 minutes. If you prefer it, one large mould could be used, about 1 pint size. For this *allow 15 minutes.*

1 can (about 8 oz or ¼ kg) salmon
1 small jar salmon-and-shrimp paste
1 small onion, grated
1 teaspoon sugar
1½ oz (38 g) fresh breadcrumbs
2 eggs, beaten
¼ pint (125 ml) cream or evaporated milk
a little pepper

1. In a bowl combine the salmon, paste, onion, sugar, breadcrumbs, beaten eggs, cream and pepper. Mix well.
2. Pour ½ pint water (¼ litre) into pressure pan and insert rack. Begin to heat.
3. Well grease 6 or 7 small metal moulds, each ⅛ pint (63 ml) size, or if you prefer it, use a larger 1-pint-sized mould, remembering to add 2 minutes extra if your mould is glass or china.
4. Tip mixture into mould or moulds. Place on rack, cover either with a piece of foil or a plate.
5. Fix lid and bring to pressure. *Allow 8 minutes for individual moulds and 15 minutes for a large one.*
6. Reduce pressure and remove lid. Lift out moulds and turn out. They may be served either hot or cold. Delicious with sliced cucumber.

SOUSED HERRINGS

Time: 6 minutes *Serves 6 or more*

Your pressure pan is particularly good at impregnating herrings with the tangy 'souse' brine. The steam holds the flavours and none can escape.

6–8 herrings
¼ pint (125 ml) vinegar
¼ pint (125 ml) water
2 level teaspoons brown sugar
1 medium-sized onion, peeled and quartered
6 peppercorns
4 cloves
1 level teaspoon salt
1 teaspoon basil
1 bay leaf

1. Clean and trim the herrings and remove heads. Place fish in pressure pan without rack.
2. Pour in the vinegar and water, then add all the other ingredients.
3. Fix lid and bring to pressure. *Allow 6 minutes.* Reduce pressure

and remove lid. Lift out herrings and leave to cool. Serve cold with salad. The 'souse' may be put away in the refrigerator and used again.

STUFFED HADDOCK WITH SAVOURY GOLDEN POTATOES

Time: 8 minutes *Serves 3–4*

The plan here is to cook the potatoes, onions and carrots together in the bottom of the pressure pan, with the fish, parcelled in foil, on the rack or trivet. Afterwards the vegetables are beaten together with butter and milk until golden and savoury.

1 fresh haddock, about 1¼–1½ lb (600–700 g)
2 teaspoons butter
1 lb (½ kg) potatoes, peeled. If large, cut in halves
2 carrots, peeled and cut into rounds
1 large or 2 smaller peeled, sliced onions
salt and a little pepper to taste

STUFFING
1 oz (25 g or ½ cup) soft breadcrumbs
½ teaspoon thyme or mixed herbs
1 small onion, peeled and grated
a dash of pepper
2 teaspoons butter

1. Ask the fishmonger to remove the backbone and trim the fish for you. Wash it well.
2. Mix together the ingredients for the stuffing. The butter is just chopped in. Push stuffing into the fish and secure with small skewers.
3. Place the vegetables in pressure pan and add ¼ pint water (125 ml) and 1 teaspoon salt. Put rack or trivet on top.
4. Spread fish with the butter and sprinkle with salt and pepper. Wrap in foil and place on rack.
5. Fix lid and bring to pressure. *Allow 8 minutes.*
6. Reduce pressure and remove lid. Lift out the fish on rack or trivet with pointed spoon. Drain liquid from vegetables and mash well with a little butter and milk. (*See Chapter 7 for a sauce.*)

FISH RISOTTO CARDINALE

Time: 5 minutes *Serves 4*

Any dish that boasts the name 'Cardinale' will be red, or at least an interesting pink. This one is coloured with tomatoes or pimentos and has an unusually tangy taste.

1 lb (½ kg) skinned boned fish of your choice, cut into 1½ in pieces
8 oz (¼ kg) or 1 cup long-grain rice (white or brown)
1 onion, peeled and finely sliced
an 8 oz (¼ kg) can of tomatoes or pimentos or fresh peeled tomatoes
½ pint (¼ litre) water
½ teaspoon basil
3 teaspoons Worcester sauce
2 teaspoons brown sugar
2 teaspoons anchovy sauce
salt and pepper to taste
grated Cheddar or Parmesan cheese

1. Put all ingredients except the cheese into pressure pan.
2. Fix lid and bring to pressure. *Allow 5 minutes.*
3. Reduce pressure and remove lid. Taste and check seasoning.
4. Tip either into a heated serving dish or into individual dishes. Sprinkle thickly with the cheese. If liked, put under the grill until cheese is sizzling.

KEDGEREE

Time: 5 minutes *Serves 4*

Together with many other recipes, Kedgeree is a reminder of our long association with India and is now an acceptable breakfast, luncheon or supper dish.

1½ lb (¾ kg) fish, preferably smoked, but fresh may be used, or canned (see Note on p. 65)
8 oz (200 g or 1 cup) long-grain rice
1 level tablespoon curry powder (or to taste)
water (see step 3)
1 bay leaf
salt if necessary
1 tablespoon butter
2 hard-boiled eggs
3 or more tablespoons top milk or cream
about 2 oz (50 g) grated Cheddar or Parmesan cheese
chopped parsley

1. If smoked fish is used, soak in plenty of water for at least ½ hour to remove excess salt. Skin and bone then flake the fish.
2. Wash rice and put into pressure pan. Stir in curry powder and the fish. Add bay leaf.
3. Allow 1¼ pints (625 ml) for fresh fish. For smoked add an extra 6 tablespoons water.
4. For fresh fish add salt to taste. For smoked, check first then add salt if necessary.
5. Fix lid and bring to pressure. *Allow 5 minutes.*
6. Reduce pressure and remove lid. Stir in the butter. Allow to stand while eggs are quartered and cheese grated. During this time the rice will absorb more of the liquid. Add enough top milk or cream to make the mixture moist. Fold in the eggs.
7. Remove bay leaf then tip mixture into serving dish. Top with the cheese and put under grill or into oven until cheese has melted and is lightly browned. Sprinkle with chopped parsley.

Note: Canned fish may be used and would be useful for an emergency. Use about half the quantity. Tuna, salmon or crab or a mixture of two would be tasty: use the liquor instead of some of the water.

JAMBALAYA

Time: 5 minutes *Serves 6–8*

Jambalaya is a famous traditional dish from America's Louisiana and is a rice mixture with a selection of meats and fish.

RICE MIXTURE

1 tablespoon butter or oil
1 Spanish onion
4 sticks of celery, cut into ½ in pieces
¾ lb (300 g or 1½ cups) long-grain rice
¾ lb (300 g) skinned tomatoes, or equivalent canned
1 small green pepper, de-seeded and cut into ¼ in strips
1 or 2 cloves of garlic, crushed
2 rounded teaspoons brown sugar
2 teaspoons tomato purée
1½ pints (¾ litre) water with 2 chicken stock cubes
½ teaspoon thyme
salt and pepper to taste

ADDITIONS

½ lb (¼ kg) cooked ham, ½ in thick
½ lb (¼ kg) cooked prawns
½ lb (¼ kg) chorizo sausage, or garlic sausage
2 tablespoons brandy
chopped parsley

1. Melt butter or oil in pressure pan. Chop onion and add. Fry gently for 2 minutes.
2. Add celery, then rice, tomatoes, pepper, garlic, sugar, tomato purée, water with cubes, thyme and seasoning. Mix well. Fix lid and bring to pressure. *Allow 5 minutes.*
3. Meanwhile melt another tablespoon butter or oil in another pan. Cut ham into ½ in cubes and add, with the prawns. Cut sausage into ½ in pieces and add. Fry for a few minutes. Pour in the warmed brandy and ignite.
4. Reduce pressure in pressure pan and remove lid. Add extra salt if necessary. Tip into heated dish and arrange the additions on top. Sprinkle with chopped parsley.

PAELLA

Times: 10 minutes, then 20 without pressure — *Serves 12*

A paella is not, strictly speaking, the actual mixture of ingredients, but the dish in which it is cooked and served. It is a large flat round vessel with straight 3 in sides and into it goes an amazing variety of fish, fowl and vegetables on a base of rice. It is Spain's main traditional dish.

2 tablespoons olive oil or butter
1 young chicken, disjointed, skinned and cut into 12 pieces
1 Spanish onion, peeled and chopped
½ pint (¼ litre) stock, or water with 1 chicken stock cube
½ lb (¼ kg) peeled sliced tomatoes
1 level tablespoon brown sugar
2 teaspoons salt and a little pepper
2 bay leaves
6 oz (150 g) piece of ham, ½ in thick and cut into ½ in cubes
½ lb (¼ kg) mushrooms, washed and halved
½ lb (¼ kg) cooked prawns
½ lb (½ kg) haddock or turbot, skinned, boned and cut into chunks
1 green pepper, deseeded and sliced

½ lb (¼ kg) can of pimentos
10 oz (250 g) long-grain rice
½ level teaspoon powdered saffron
2 cloves of garlic, crushed
about 20 fresh mussels (or a jar of mussels, any size)
chopped parsley

1. Heat oil or butter in pressure can. Add chicken and onion and fry together for about 5 minutes. Remove pan from heat.
2. Add stock, tomatoes, brown sugar, seasoning and bay leaves. Fix lid and bring to pressure. *Allow 10 minutes.*
3. Meanwhile fry in 1 tablespoon butter the ham and mushrooms. After 10 minutes, add the prawns and let them heat through.
4. Reduce pressure and remove lid of pressure pan.
5. Add the haddock, green pepper, pimentos, rice, saffron and cloves of garlic.
6. Cook without pressure for about 20 minutes, or until rice has softened. Add a little more water as rice swells.
7. Add the ham, mushrooms and prawns. Add more seasoning if necessary (*see step 8*).
8. If mussels are to be used, wash them well and put into another saucepan with 6 tablespoons water and a bay leaf (half wine may be used). Cook for about 5 minutes until they open, and discard any that don't. If ready-prepared mussels are to be used, add the liquor to the mixture in step 5 and add mussels with the ham etc.
9. To serve, remove bay leaves and tip mixture into 1 or 2 casseroles. Arrange mussels on top and keep hot in the oven. Sprinkle with chopped parsley just before serving.

SPAGHETTI ALLA BOLOGNESE

Times: 8 minutes each for spaghetti and sauce — *Serves 4*

There are two ways of preparing this tasty dish. The spaghetti could be cooked in an ordinary saucepan and the sauce in the pressure pan. Or the sauce could be cooked first in the pressure pan, then tipped into a saucepan ready for reheating, and the pressure pan washed and used for the spaghetti.

8–10 oz (200–250 g) long spaghetti or 1 lb (½ kg) if you want second helpings
2½ pints (1¼ litres) water
1 teaspoon salt
1 level tablespoon butter

SAUCE

3 rashers streaky bacon
1 large onion, finely chopped
1 level tablespoon flour
1 lb (½ kg) minced beef
3–4 peeled tomatoes
¼ pint (125 ml) water
2 teaspoons paprika
½ teaspoon thyme or dried herbs
2 teaspoons Worcester sauce
1 teaspoon sugar
salt and pepper to taste (2 teaspoons soy sauce may replace some of the salt)
1 clove of garlic, crushed (optional)
grated Cheddar or Parmesan cheese

1. For the first method suggested above, start cooking the spaghetti with the water and salt in an ordinary saucepan, then make the sauce in the pressure pan.
2. Remove rinds from bacon, cut into 1 in pieces and drop into pressure pan. Add onion and fry together for a few minutes while fat runs out of bacon.
3. Add beef and flour and mix in with the bacon and onions.
4. Add tomatoes, water, paprika, herb, Worcester sauce, sugar, seasoning and garlic. Mix well together.
5. Fix lid and bring to pressure. *Allow 8 minutes.*
6. Reduce pressure and remove lid. Keep hot until spaghetti has cooked, it will take about 15–20 minutes. Strain spaghetti and add the butter. Stir until well coated.
7. If you have decided to cook the spaghetti in the pressure pan, keep sauce hot in another saucepan, wash the pressure pan and cook the spaghetti for *8 minutes at pressure.* Reduce pressure, remove lid and strain. Add the butter.
8. To serve, put a helping of spaghetti on to each heated plate and cover with the sauce. Sprinkle generously with the cheese.

SPAGHETTI IN TOMATO SAUCE

Time: 8 minutes *Serves 6*

If the family get through canned spaghetti in tomato sauce at an alarming rate, why not try your own and save money? All the ingredients go into the pressure pan at once and in a few minutes the commercial kind has a serious rival.

1 lb (½ kg) tomatoes
1 level tablespoon butter or margarine
2 level tablespoons flour
1½ pints (¾ litre) water
1 tablespoon tomato ketchup
2 rashers streaky bacon
1 bay leaf
2 level teaspoons salt and a little pepper
¾ lb (300 g) spaghetti
1 or 2 level tablespoons sugar (see step 3)

1. Skin and slice the tomatoes.
2. Melt the butter in pressure pan and add flour. Cook together for ½ minute, then tip in the tomatoes. Mix well.
3. Add water, ketchup, bacon, bay leaf, seasoning, spaghetti and sugar. Tomatoes need sugar to enhance their flavour; if they are tart, add the 2 level tablespoons.
4. Stir together. Fix lid and bring to pressure. *Allow 8 minutes.*
5. Reduce pressure and remove lid. Take out bacon and bay leaf. Add more seasoning if necessary.

Note: The spaghetti could be broken into 3 or 4 in lengths before cooking.

BAKED BEANS

Total time: 45 or 55 minutes (see step 2) *Serves 6*

As with the preceding recipe, the family can enjoy your own home cooking with a considerable saving in the shopping bills.

6 oz (150 g) haricot or other small dried beans
1¼ pints (625 ml) water with 1 teaspoon salt
1 medium-sized onion, peeled and finely chopped
½ lb (¼ kg) tomatoes, peeled and sliced, or a small can of tomato soup (10 oz or 250 g approx.)
2 level teaspoons salt and a little pepper
2 level tablespoons brown sugar

1 good tablespoon golden syrup or treacle
2 rashers bacon
1 teaspoon made mustard
1 tablespoon concentrated tomato purée
3 rounded teaspoons flour (2 if soup is used)

1. Soak the beans in the water and salt for about 6 hours or longer. (If you wish to make the baked beans at once, omit the soaking and pressure-cook for an extra 10 minutes. See next step.)
2. Tip the soaked beans and water into pressure pan and fix lid. Bring to pressure and *allow 10 minutes.* If beans were not soaked, *allow 20 minutes.*
3. Have ready a dish about 3 in deep that will fit comfortably into your pressure pan. No need to grease it.
4. While the beans are pressure-cooking, put into this dish the onion, tomatoes or soup, the seasoning, sugar, syrup, bacon (rind removed) cut into ½ in pieces, mustard and tomato purée. Sprinkle in the flour and mix it into the ingredients.
5. When time is up, reduce pressure and remove lid. Strain off the water (save it for soup). Tip the beans into the dish with the other ingredients and mix together.
6. Put 1 pint (½ litre) water into pressure pan and insert rack or trivet. Begin to heat.
7. Cover dish with foil and secure with string or a rubber band. Put on the rack in pressure pan. Fix lid and bring to pressure. *Allow 35 minutes.*
8. Reduce pressure and remove lid. Take out dish and remove foil. Taste and check seasoning.

CHICORY AND HAM ROLLS

Time: 6 minutes for chicory *Serves 4*

The chicory is cooked first in the pressure pan, then it is split open, filled with a mushroom and onion filling, and wrapped in a slice of ham.

½ pint (¼ litre) salted water
4 heads of chicory
2 teaspoons butter or margarine
1 onion, peeled and finely chopped
4 oz (100 g) mushrooms, washed and chopped

¼ teaspoon salt and a little pepper
4 slices of thinly cut ham
cheese sauce (p. 192)
chopped parsley

1. Pour ½ pint (¼ litre) water into the pressure pan and add ½ teaspoon salt. Put in the rack and place the chicory on it.
2. Fix lid and bring to pressure. *Allow 6 minutes.*
3. Meanwhile melt the butter or margarine in a small frying-pan. Add the onions and cook gently until they are transparent. Add the mushrooms. Fry together until the onions have softened. Season with salt and pepper.
4. Reduce pressure in pan and remove lid. Lift out the chicory. Split each 'chicon' half-way through lengthwise then push a little of the onion and mushroom mixture into each.
5. Press closed again and wrap each in the ham. Arrange side by side in an ovenproof dish. Keep warm, covered, in oven while the sauce is being made. If you have no oven, let them steam on top of the pressure pan, covered with an enamel plate.
6. Pour the sauce over the rolls and sprinkle with chopped parsley.

CHEESE CUSTARD

Time: 7 minutes *Serves 2*

A basic Cheese Custard that may be varied in many ways. Three savoury ideas are given and you will no doubt invent many more.

2 medium eggs
2 or 3 oz (50–75 g) cheese (grated Cheddar or Parmesan)
½ pint (¼ litre) warm milk
½ teaspoon salt and a little pepper
½ teaspoon sugar

1. Pour ½ pint (¼ litre) water into pressure pan and insert rack or trivet. Begin to heat.
2. Have ready a dish about 2–2½ in deep that will fit comfortably into the pan. Grease it with butter or margarine.
3. Beat the eggs and add the cheese, milk and seasoning and sugar. Pour into the dish. Cover it with foil and secure with string or a rubber band.
4. Lower dish on to rack. Fix lid and bring to pressure. *Allow 7 minutes.*

5. Move pan to a cool surface and let the pressure reduce gradually. Remove lid and lift out the custard.

Cheese custard, larger size: To serve 4, use 3 large eggs, ¾ pint milk (375 ml), 5 oz (125 g) grated cheese, and extra seasoning. *Allow 12 minutes.*

Savoury cheese custard: For either size, add 2–3 teaspoons French capers and about 2 teaspoons chopped olives or gherkins, or both.

Cheese and ham custard: Add 2–3 oz (50–75 g) chopped ham.

Cheese custard with tomato: Replace the milk with the same quantity of skinned chopped tomatoes or Italian canned tomatoes. Increase sugar to 1 heaped teaspoon.

CAULIFLOWER CHEESE CUSTARD

Time: 9 minutes *Serves 2–3*

A vegetarian dish that would make a light, nourishing meal for an invalid or convalescent and a change from meat for the fighting fit.

2 medium eggs
¼ pint (125 ml) milk
about ¼ lb (¼ kg) chopped, cooked cauliflower
2–3 oz (50–75 g) grated Cheddar or Parmesan cheese
½ teaspoon salt and a little pepper (celery salt could be used)

1. Pour ½ pint (¼ litre) water into pressure pan and begin to heat. Insert rack or trivet.
2. Have ready a dish about 2½ in deep that will fit comfortably in the pressure pan. Grease it with butter or margarine.
3. Beat the eggs and add the milk, cauliflower, cheese and seasoning. Tip into the dish. Cover it with foil and secure with string or a rubber band.
4. Lower dish on to rack.
5. Fix lid and bring to pressure. *Allow 9 minutes.*
6. Move pan to a cool surface and let the pressure reduce gradually.

MACARONI CHEESE CUSTARD

Time: 12 minutes *Serves 3*

A macaroni cheese that is lighter than the traditional one and therefore ideal for an invalid.

about 8 oz (200 g) cooked macaroni, noodles or spaghetti
2 large eggs
3 oz (75 g) grated Cheddar or Parmesan cheese
½ pint (¼ litre) milk
salt and pepper to taste
chopped parsley or chives (optional)

1. Have ready a dish about 2–2½ in deep that will fit comfortably into the pressure pan. Grease it with butter or margarine.
2. See that the macaroni is well drained.
3. Beat the eggs in the dish, then add the cheese, milk and seasoning. Add the parsley or chives if liked. Mix well. Add the macaroni.
4. Put ½ pint (¼ litre) water into pressure pan. Insert rack or trivet and begin to heat.
5. Cover dish with foil and secure with a rubber band or string. Lower into pressure pan.
6. Fix lid and bring to pressure. *Allow 12 minutes.*
7. Remove pan to a cool surface and let the pressure reduce gradually. Remove lid and lift out the custard.

Rice cheese custard: Use 6 oz (150 g) cooked rice instead of the macaroni.

SWEETCORN, TOMATO AND CHEESE CUSTARD

Time: 12 minutes *Serves 3–4*

Three flavours that blend well to produce a quick meatless meal.

2 large eggs
3 small tomatoes, peeled (about 6 oz or 150 g)
3 oz (75 g) grated Cheddar or Parmesan cheese
1 teaspoon sugar
an 8 oz (200 g) can of cream-style sweetcorn
½ teaspoon salt and a little pepper
1 teaspoon Worcester sauce (optional)

1. Have ready a dish about 2–2½ in deep that will fit comfortably into the pan.
2. Beat the eggs and add the tomatoes, cheese, sugar, sweetcorn and seasoning, including Worcester sauce if liked.
3. Tip into the dish. Cover with foil and secure with a rubber band or string.
4. Pour ½ pint (¼ litre) of water into pressure pan and insert trivet. Lower dish on to it.
5. Fix lid and bring to pressure. *Allow 12 minutes.*
6. Remove pan to a cool surface and let pressure reduce gradually. Remove lid and lift out the custard.

HORS D'OEUVRE SAVOURY CUSTARDS

Time: 3 minutes *Serves 6*

For a dinner or luncheon party first course, quickly made little individual hors d'oeuvre darioles may be created from the preceding custard recipes, or using ingredients of your own choice. Give them their 3 minutes while the guests are chatting over their drinks, then leave them while the pressure reduces gradually. Leave the lid on the pressure pan until you are ready to serve dinner. The custards will keep warm without further cooking.

1. Grease well six dariole moulds or other small containers such as old teacups, about 1½–2 in deep. If they are smaller, you might need 8.
2. Pour ¼ pint (125 ml) water into pressure pan and insert rack.
3. The darioles are placed in two layers in the pressure pan. Put the first layer on the rack and cover with a double thickness of aluminium foil. Repeat layer.
4. Fix lid and bring to pressure. *Allow 3 minutes.*
5. Move the pan from heat and leave on a cold surface while pressure reduces gradually. Leave the lid on the pan until you want to serve the savouries. Sprinkle with chopped parsley, or put one sprig on each.

LENTIL CROQUETTES AND CUTLETS

Time: 15 minutes *Serves 4*

The part played by the pressure cooker in these recipes makes a useful contribution to time and fuel-saving. Instead of having first to soak the lentils then cook them for an hour in an ordinary saucepan, the pressure pan will transform them to a mush without soaking and in only 15 minutes.

6 oz (150 g) lentils, or 6 barely rounded tablespoons
1½ gills (188 ml) water
1 medium-sized onion, peeled and finely chopped or grated
plenty of salt and pepper
a pinch of thyme

1. Have ready a 1½ pint (¾ litre) bowl or dish that will fit comfortably in the pressure pan.
2. Wash the lentils in a fine sieve and put into the bowl.
3. Add the water, onion, seasoning and thyme. Stir together.
4. Put ¾ pint (375 ml) water into pressure pan. Insert rack and begin to heat.
5. Cover bowl with foil and secure with a rubber band or string. Place dish on the rack.
6. Fix lid and bring to pressure. *Allow 15 minutes.*
7. Reduce pressure and remove lid. Lift out the bowl and remove foil.

Lentil croquettes: Add to the mashed lentils 1 beaten standard egg, 4 oz (100 g) cheese, either grated Cheddar or Parmesan, or a soft cheese such as Roquefort, Philadelphia or a Gruyere. Or substitute for the cheese about 2 oz (50 g) finely chopped walnuts or other nuts. 2 or 3 tablespoons breadcrumbs may be added. Season with salt and pepper. Form into croquettes and roll in flour or fine dry breadcrumbs. Fry in hot fat until browned all over. The quantity makes 8 croquettes 5 in long.

Lentil cutlets: Flatten mixture into cutlet shapes, coat with flour or fine breadcrumbs and fry.

EGGS WITH LENTIL SAUCE AND BROWN RICE

Time: 12 minutes *Serves 3–4*

The sauce and rice are cooked at the same time in the pressure pan, and the eggs separately in a small saucepan. An intriguing dish.

THE SAUCE

4 oz (100 g) lentils or 4 barely rounded tablespoons
¾ pint (375 ml) hot water
½ bay leaf
1 rasher streaky bacon
1 level teaspoon salt and a little pepper

THE RICE

8 oz (¼ kg or 1 cup) brown rice
1 pint (½ litre) water
1 level teaspoon salt and a little pepper
½ chicken stock cube could be crumbled and added to give extra flavour (optional)

1 or 2 eggs per serving
chopped parsley (optional)

1. Wash the lentils through a fine sieve and put into pressure pan. Add water, bay leaf, bacon and seasoning.
2. Have ready a 2 pint (1 litre) bowl that will fit comfortably in the pressure pan. Wash the rice in the sieve and put into the bowl. Add the water and seasoning, also the cube if liked.
3. Cover the bowl tightly with foil and secure with a rubber band or string. Put into pressure pan with the lentils.
4. Fix lid and bring to pressure. *Allow 12 minutes.*
5. Meanwhile hard-boil any number of eggs you wish.
6. Reduce pressure and remove lid. Lift out bowl and take off the foil. Take out the bay leaf and rasher and stir the sauce well.
7. Shell the eggs and cut in halves lengthwise. Place on a well-warmed serving dish or individual plates. Pour the sauce over the eggs and surround with the rice. The rasher could be cut into tiny pieces and sprinkled over the top. Chopped parsley would make an attractive finish.

Curried eggs with lentil sauce: At step 1 add 1 level tablespoon curry powder to the lentils. Add also 1 teaspoon brown sugar.

PEASE PUDDING

Time: 28 minutes *Serves 4–5*

This is an English regional dish, popularly served with hot ham, bacon or pork.

8 oz (¼ kg) pink dried split peas
½ pint (¼ litre) water plus 4 tablespoons
1 level teaspoon salt and a little pepper
a few left-over bacon rinds or 1 rasher bacon
fine dry breadcrumbs

1. Have ready a 2 pint (1 litre) bowl or dish that will fit comfortably into the pressure pan and can also be brought to the table.
2. Wash the peas through a fine strainer and tip into bowl. Add the water, seasoning and rinds or rasher.
3. Pour 1 pint (½ litre) water into pressure pan and insert rack. Begin to heat.
4. Cover the bowl or dish with foil and secure tightly with string or a rubber band. Place the dish on the rack.
5. Fix lid and bring to pressure. *Allow 28 minutes.*
6. Reduce pressure and remove lid. Lift out bowl and remove foil. Sprinkle with the breadcrumbs. The pudding should be smooth and as stiff as mashed potatoes. As it cools it will become stiffer and may be cut into slices.

Pease pudding slices fried with bacon: Make the pease pudding and when cold cut into ½ in slices. Fry some bacon first, then the slices in the hot bacon fat. An inexpensive and nutritious breakfast dish.

EGGS AND CHEESE IN CHESTNUT SAUCE

Time: 13 minutes altogether *Serves 3–4*

Chestnuts have tough skins, so first the pressure pan must soften them for peeling. After that the sauce and hard-boiled eggs are cooked in the pan itself and the sauce in a bowl. A tempting and nourishing vegetarian dish.

½ lb (¼ kg) chestnuts
½ pint (¼ litre) milk
1 teaspoon dried onion
2 teaspoons butter
½ teaspoon salt and a little pepper
½ bay leaf
1–2 eggs per serving
2 oz (50 g) grated Cheddar or Parmesan cheese
chopped parsley

1. Prepare and cook chestnuts as described on *p. 38*.
2. Have ready a 1½ or 2 pint (¾ or 1 litre) bowl and crumble the chestnuts into it. Add the milk, onions, butter, seasoning and bay leaf. Cover with foil and secure with string or a rubber band.
3. Put ½ pint (¼ litre) water into pressure pan and begin to heat.
4. Put 3 or 4 of the eggs in their shells into the water in the pan, around the outside. Arrange the bowl in the centre. Put a small plate on it. The rest of the eggs could go on the plate.
5. Fix the lid and bring to pressure. *Allow 7 minutes.*
6. Reduce pressure and remove lid. Remove the eggs, then take out the bowl. Remove foil. Push the sauce through a sieve into a small saucepan or an ovenproof dish. Stir sauce to a creamy consistency. Add more seasoning if necessary.
7. Shell the eggs and cut in halves lengthwise. Add to the sauce. If using the ovenproof dish, sprinkle with the cheese and reheat in the oven or under the grill. If using the saucepan, reheat, then put on to individual plates. Sprinkle each with the cheese and garnish if liked with parsley.

VEGETARIAN RICE LOAF

Times: 30 minutes *Serves 6*
(3 minutes for rice if not cooked in advance)

A new and interesting vegetarian loaf that may be served either hot with vegetables, cold with a salad, or packed into the picnic basket.

¾ lb (600 g) cooked rice (see step 2)
2 oz (50 g or 1 cup) soft bread-crumbs
1 onion, grated
4 or more oz (100 g) grated Cheddar or Parmesan cheese or any well-flavoured cheese of your choice

1 small green pepper, de-seeded and chopped
2 large or 3 small eggs, beaten
¼ pint (125 ml) milk
1 or more tablespoons chopped parsley
salt and pepper to taste

1. Have ready a tin about 3 in deep that will fit comfortably into your pressure pan. If a loaf-shaped one will not fit, use a deep 7 in cake tin.
2. To obtain ¾ lb cooked rice, allow 6 oz (150 g) uncooked rice and ¾ pint (375 ml) water and pressure-cook for 3 minutes, as described on *p. 198*. Drain well.
3. Combine in a mixing bowl the rice, breadcrumbs, onion, cheese, green pepper, beaten eggs, milk, parsley and seasoning.
4. Put 1 pint (½ litre) water into pressure pan and insert rack. Begin to heat.
5. Tip mixture into greased tin and press down evenly. Cover with foil and secure with string or a rubber band. Place on rack in pressure pan.
6. Fix lid and bring to pressure. *Allow 30 minutes.*
7. Reduce pressure and remove lid. Lift out tin and remove foil. Loosen the sides and turn out. Garnish with slices of tomato and sprigs of parsley.

VEGETARIAN CURRY AND RICE

Times: 5 minutes for vegetables
3–5 minutes for rice

Serves 4

Served with cheese and a green vegetable this would make a satisfying main dish. It provides a good balance of vegetables, protein and starch.

about 6 sticks celery, or one small head, cleaned and chopped into ½ in pieces
2 or 3 leeks, cleaned and sliced
1 Spanish onion (or 2 English), peeled and finely chopped
4–6 tomatoes, peeled
1 can of carrots, any size
1 teaspoon brown sugar
salt and pepper to taste
10 oz (250 g or 1¼ cup) rice

CURRY SAUCE

1 tablespoon butter or margarine
3–5 teaspoons curry powder
1½ level tablespoons wholemeal flour
1 or more teaspoons vegetable concentrate
4–6 tablespoons soured cream

1. Wash and trim celery and leeks and cut into ½ in pieces. Put into pressure pan. Add the onion and the tomatoes.
2. Open can of carrots. Measure juice and if it is less than ½ pint (¼ litre), make it up with water. Add liquid to vegetables. (Do not add the carrots.) Add sugar and seasoning.
3. Fix lid and bring to pressure. *Allow 5 minutes.*
4. Reduce pressure and remove lid. Strain the liquid into a bowl and put the vegetables into an ovenproof dish. Slice the carrots and add. Cover dish and keep warm.
5. Wash pressure pan and cook the rice in it (*see p. 198*). Add a little more salt if necessary.
6. For the curry sauce, melt the butter or margarine in a small pan. Add the curry powder and flour and cook for 2 minutes. Remove from heat and add the vegetable concentrate, then whisk in the vegetable water. Return to heat and cook until smooth. Add salt and pepper and the soured cream. Pour this sauce over the vegetables. Serve with the rice.

3. Meat, Poultry and Game

All dishes suitable for a saucepan or casserole are possible in the pressure saucepan and the recipes that follow will show how enormous is the range. They not only cover the familiar dishes to which we are all accustomed, but also include some that are more unusual. By running through the index under the headings of Meats and Poultry, it will be obvious that in the chapter there is something for everyone for all occasions.

Many people avoid buying the cheaper cuts of meats because of the long hours of cooking needed to make them tender. With the pressure pan, the toughest meats may be cooked in a fraction of the time. If cut ½–1 in thick, they will cook to perfect tenderness in one quarter of the usual time and in one large piece, a pot roast for instance, will cook in half the time. Indeed, a full-flavoured stew made of inexpensive meat may be cooked after a day away from home and be on the table in less than ½ hour.

GRAVY

Because liquid is not steamed away as in conventional methods, pressure-cooked dishes retain all that you have put in, including the juices from the meat and vegetables. This means that when you open the pan, you will probably find more gravy than you had expected. In the majority of the following recipes, ½ pint (¼ litre) of stock or water has been suggested. If this forms more gravy than you wish, reduce this amount down to 1½ gills (188 ml) or ¼ pint (125 ml) (*do not reduce to less than the ¼ pint*) and use only half the usual amount of flour for thickening.

COOKING TIMES FOR MEAT AND POULTRY

Meat and poultry sold in both supermarkets and butchers' shops, are, as a rule, of 'average' age and it is in this condition that the times for pressure-cooking are given in the following chapter.

The exact age of lamb is seldom revealed to the housewife. In some countries, the butcher classifies it as 'spring lamb', 'hogget' (1–1½ year old lamb) and mutton. But in England the word 'lamb' covers everything, except perhaps really old animals. A few minutes less pressure-cooking time than suggested should be given for young spring lamb, but even this should be well cooked.

So far as beef is concerned, only the very expensive cuts may be underdone and these are rarely subjected to pressure-cooking. I have, however, given timings for rump steak in some of the beef recipes as you may prefer to use this on special occasions.

Really young chickens should be given less pressure-cooking time than suggested in the recipes. For instance, poussins, 4–8 weeks old, would need only 8–12 minutes, cooked whole; and spring chickens, about 2–3 months old, 15 minutes if whole and 12 minutes if disjointed.

Meat

BEEF STEW, BASIC RECIPE

Time: 25 minutes *Serves 4*

Tenderness is essential if a beef stew is to be enjoyed. Next in importance is the flavour of the gravy: this may be varied greatly according to taste. See below for suggestions.

1 lb (½ kg) stewing steak
1 level tablespoon butter, margarine or oil
2 medium onions, peeled and chopped
1½ level tablespoons flour
½ pint (¼ litre) stock, or water with 1 beef stock cube
½ teaspoon thyme
2 or 3 carrots, cleaned and sliced or halved
salt and pepper to taste (2 teaspoons soy sauce may replace some of the salt)

1. Wash and trim steak and cut into 1 in cubes.
2. Heat fat in the pressure pan and add onions.
3. Add meat and fry with onions for 3 minutes. Add flour and toss about for 2 minutes, then remove from heat.
4. Add liquid, thyme, carrots and seasoning. Return to heat and mix well.
5. Fix lid and bring to pressure. *Allow times shown above.*
6. Reduce pressure and remove lid. Check seasoning before serving.

Beef stew with tomatoes: Add 3 or 4 skinned tomatoes and 1 teaspoon sugar. Replace thyme with basil.

Beef stew with pickled walnuts: Add 4–6 pickled walnuts, quartered, and 2 teaspoons brown sugar.

Beef stew with packet soups: Choose any flavour of soup—asparagus, celery, mushroom or any other that takes your fancy. Follow the basic recipe but use 1 heaped tablespoon of the soup powder instead of the flour. If you choose tomato, be sure to add 1 or 2 teaspoons sugar.

BEEF OLIVES

Time: 16 minutes *Serves 6*

When buying meat for these rolls (beef olives), let the butcher know what you are planning to cook and he will cut thin slices of meat the right size, then beat them out until they are about 4 in × 5 in and no more than $\frac{1}{8}$ in thick.

ROLLS

About 1½ lb (¾ kg) topside or rump steak (see above)
2 level tablespoons flour
2 level tablespoons fat
1 medium-sized onion, peeled and chopped
a few mushrooms, washed and chopped (optional)
½ pint plus 4 tablespoons (approx. 300 ml) water, or part water, part red wine
2 teaspoons soy sauce or 1 beef stock cube
salt and pepper to taste

STUFFING

3 oz (75 g or 1½ cups) fresh breadcrumbs
1 teaspoon fresh or ½ teaspoon dried thyme or mixed herbs
1 small onion, peeled and grated
½ teaspoon salt and a little pepper
2 teaspoons soft butter

1. For the stuffing, combine the crumbs, herbs, onion and seasoning. Roughly chop in the butter. (Do not add liquid or egg.)
2. Spread a little stuffing on each slice of meat and roll up. Secure with thread, tiny skewers or cocktail picks. Roll in the flour.
3. Melt the fat in the pressure pan and fry the rolls until lightly browned. Remove them to a plate.
4. Add onion to the pan and fry for 2 minutes, together with the mushrooms, if liked. Remove from heat and add the liquid, soy sauce or stock cube and the seasoning. Stir well then return to heat.
   Put the rolls back. Fix lid and bring to pressure. *Allow 16 minutes.* Reduce pressure and remove lid. Remove fastening from rolls. Check gravy for seasoning.

TIPSY BEEF OR VEAL ROLLS

Time: 16 minutes *Serves 6*

A dinner-party dish with a difference. The rolls are filled with sherry-flavoured dates and small pieces of bacon. Sherry also flavours the gravy. As with the previous recipe, ask your butcher to beat the meat to not more than ⅛ in thick. Fillet of veal can be used instead of beef.

4 oz (100 g) stoned dates
7 tablespoons sherry
1½ lb (¾ kg) sliced rump steak or veal fillet (see above)
6 bacon rashers
2 tablespoons butter or other fat
1½ level tablespoons flour
about 6 oz (150 g) onions, peeled and chopped
½ pint (¼ litre) stock, or water with 1 chicken or beef cube
2 teaspoons paprika pepper (not cayenne!)
salt and pepper to taste
1 clove of garlic, crushed (optional)
a few mushrooms for garnish, washed and halved (optional)

1. Chop the dates and put into a small saucepan. Add 3 tablespoons of sherry and bring to the boil. Remove from heat and mash.
2. Spread a little filling on each thin slice of meat. Cover with half a rindless bacon rasher. Roll up and secure with thread, tiny skewers or cocktail picks.
3. Melt fat in pressure pan. Cover rolls with flour. Fry for a few minutes until lightly browned. Lift out and put on to a plate.
4. Add onions and fry for 2 minutes, then add stock, remaining sherry, paprika, and seasoning, including garlic if used. Mix well.
5. Put the rolls back. Fix lid and bring to pressure. *Allow 16 minutes.* If you are using mushrooms, fry them in a little butter while the meat is cooking and use as a garnish with parsley.
6. Reduce pressure and remove lid. Remove fastening from rolls. Taste gravy and add more seasoning if necessary.

BEEF OR VEAL ROLLS WITH PRUNES AND BACON

Time: 16 minutes *Serves 4*

This is similar to the Tipsy Rolls in the preceding recipe, but with a different filling and gravy. Have the meat beaten to $\frac{1}{8}$ in thick. Fillet of veal can be used instead of beef.

6 oz (150 g) cooked, stoned prunes
4 rashers of bacon
about 1$\frac{1}{4}$ lb (600 g) sliced rump steak $\frac{1}{8}$ in thick or veal fillet
2 tablespoons butter or other fat
2 onions, peeled and sliced
1$\frac{1}{2}$ level tablespoons flour
2 or more carrots (optional)
$\frac{1}{2}$ lb ($\frac{1}{4}$ kg) peeled, sliced tomatoes or a can of Italian peeled ones
$\frac{1}{4}$ pint (125 ml) syrup from the prunes
$\frac{1}{2}$ teaspoon basil or thyme
4 tablespoons water
1 clove of garlic, crushed (optional)
salt and pepper to taste
parsley

1. Cook prunes as on *p. 168*. Remove rinds and cut bacon into 3 in pieces.
2. Cut meat slices into pieces about 3$\frac{1}{2}$ in × 5 in. Place a piece of bacon on each, then 2 flattened prunes. Roll up and secure with thread, small skewers or cocktail picks.

3. Heat fat in pressure pan. Fry the rolls until lightly browned then remove them to a plate.
4. Add onions to pan and fry for 2 minutes then stir in the flour and mix well. Remove pan from heat and add the tomatoes, prune syrup, basil, water, garlic and seasoning. Stir well and return to heat.
5. Put the rolls back and add carrots if liked. Fix lid and bring to pressure. *Allow 16 minutes.*
6. Reduce pressure and remove lid. Lift out rolls and remove fastening. Add more seasoning to gravy if necessary. Serve rolls with the gravy poured over. Garnish with parsley.

BEEF STROGANOFF

Time: 12 minutes *Serves 6*

A Russian dish that has established itself in the West. Its distinguishing features are the thin strips of meat, the addition of soured cream and the flavouring of nutmeg.

1½ lb (700 g) topside or bladebone steak, cut into ⅛ in thick slices
1 level tablespoon butter or oil
1 medium-sized onion, peeled and chopped finely
2 level tablespoons flour
½ lb (¼ kg) button mushrooms, washed
½ pint (¼ litre) water with 1 beef stock cube or 2 teaspoons soy sauce
⅛ teaspoon nutmeg
salt and pepper to taste
potatoes (optional)
1 clove of garlic, crushed (optional)
¼ pint (125 ml) soured cream, or fresh cream with 2 teaspoons lemon juice

1. Trim any fat from the meat before cutting it into 1 in strips about 3–4 in long.
2. Melt fat in pressure pan and add meat and onions. Fry for about 3 minutes, then mix in the flour. Remove from heat.
3. Add mushrooms, water with stock cube or soy sauce, the nutmeg and seasoning. Mix well and return to heat. If liked, whole potatoes may be added, also the garlic.
4. Fix lid and bring to pressure. *Allow 12 minutes.*

5. Reduce pressure and remove lid.
6. Lift out potatoes if they have been included, then stir in the soured cream. Check gravy for seasoning.

BOEUF PARISIENNE

Times: 25 minutes for stewing steak
20 minutes for rump *Serves 4*

A goulash-type of beef stew, cooked in the pressure pan, then tipped into a casserole and topped with toasted French bread spread with Marmite. The gravy is subtly flavoured with dark brown ale, mushrooms and herbs.

1 tablespoon oil or other fat
1½ lb (700 g) stewing or other steak cut into serving-sized pieces about ¾ in thick
1½ level tablespoons flour
2 medium-sized onions, peeled and sliced
4 oz (100 g) mushrooms, washed and halved
½ pint (¼ litre) dark brown ale
½ level teaspoon mixed herbs or any herb of your choice
1 clove of garlic, crushed (optional)
salt and pepper to taste
8 slices of French bread buttered and spread with Marmite
parsley

1. Melt oil or fat in pressure pan.
2. Trim any fat or gristle from the meat, then coat with the flour. Fry in the fat until lightly browned, then remove to a plate.
3. Add onions to pan and fry for 1 minute, add the mushrooms and toss and cook with the onions for another 2 minutes.
4. Remove from heat and add the ale, herbs and the garlic if used. Put the meat back. Season with salt and pepper.
5. Fix lid and bring to pressure. *Allow times shown above.*
6. Reduce pressure and remove lid. Tip contents into a casserole. Arrange the bread slices on top and press down a little so that the underside of the bread has soaked up some of the gravy. Put under a heated grill until the edges of the bread are crisp. Garnish with parsley, either in sprigs or chopped.

BOEUF À LA BOURGUIGNONNE

Time: 25 minutes *Serves 6*

Of all the Burgundian dishes, this is probably the most famous. Burgundy is famed for its wine and also for the traditional recipes in which it is used. This one would be ideal for a winter buffet supper.

a ½ lb (200 g) slice bacon ½ in thick
1 lb (½ kg) topside beef
1½ level tablespoons flour
1 Spanish onion, or 2 smaller English ones, peeled and sliced
½ pint (¼ litre) red Burgundy
2 carrots, washed and sliced
4 oz (100 g) mushrooms, washed and halved
½ teaspoon dried bouquet garni
1 crushed clove of garlic
salt and pepper to taste

1. Remove the rind and cut the bacon into 1 in pieces. Drop into pressure pan and begin to fry.
2. Trim the steak and cut it into 1 in pieces and add to bacon. Fry for 2 minutes, then sprinkle in the flour and fry for another minute.
3. Add onions and cook and mix well. Remove from heat and add the Burgundy, carrots, mushrooms, herbs, garlic and seasoning.
4. Stir together then return to heat. Fix lid and bring to pressure. *Allow 25 minutes.*
5. Reduce pressure and remove lid. Check seasoning before serving.

HUNGARIAN GOULASH

Time: 25 minutes *Serves 6*

Austria, Germany and Hungary all have their traditional goulash, a rich beef stew flavoured with onions, paprika and garlic. In some countries a chicken goulash is made, based on the same flavours.

1½–2 lb (¾–1 kg) stewing steak
1½ level tablespoons flour
2 tablespoons oil or other fat
4 medium-sized onions, peeled and sliced
1 clove of garlic, crushed (optional)
⅛ pint (63 ml) stock, or water with 2 teaspoons soy sauce or 1 beef cube
¼ pint (125 ml) red wine

2 teaspoons mild paprika
pinch thyme
2 or 3 tomatoes, skinned and sliced

1. Trim any fat or gristle from the meat and then cut it into 1 in pieces and roll in the flour.
2. Melt the oil or fat in pressure pan. Add onions, and fry for 2 minutes. Add meat and toss around for another minute. Remove from heat.
3. Add garlic if liked, liquid, paprika, thyme and tomatoes. Mix well.
4. Fix lid and bring to pressure. *Allow 25 minutes.*
5. Reduce pressure and remove lid. Check seasoning.

Goulash with soured cream: Omit the tomatoes. When cooked and the lid removed, stir in about 4 tablespoons soured cream.

BEEF CHOP SUEY

Time: 10 minutes *Serves 4*

Once upon a time, so the story goes, in a Chinese restaurant in the U.S.A. the word 'Chop Suey' was used by mistake and since then the Chinese, not wishing to lose face, allowed it to remain. It is not used in China. After all, it means 'dirty mixed fragments'!

¾ lb (300 g) good stewing beef
3 tablespoons sherry
2 tablespoons soy sauce
⅛ teaspoon monosodium glutamate (Accent)
1 clove of garlic, crushed
1 cup of finely sliced stalk of cauliflower
¼ pint (125 ml) stock, or water with 1 chicken stock cube
10 oz (250 g) long-grain rice
1 tablespoon butter or oil
1 large Spanish onion, peeled and sliced
4 or 5 sticks of celery, trimmed and cut into ½ in pieces
12 oz (300 g) can of bean sprouts (or approximate size)
2 level teaspoons arrowroot
salt and pepper to taste

1. Trim any unwanted fat and gristle from the meat, cut it into 2 in lengths then cut the lengths into ⅛ in slices. Put them into a bowl and cover with the sherry and soy sauce. Add Accent and garlic. Allow to marinate for a few hours or overnight.

2. Tip into pressure pan, then add the cauliflower stalks and the stock. Fix lid and bring to pressure. *Allow 10 minutes.*
3. Meanwhile cook the rice in 2 pints (1 litre) of water, adding 1 good teaspoon salt. Boil rapidly for 5 minutes then cover and allow to stand and swell for 10 minutes or so.
4. At the same time heat the butter or oil in yet another pan then add the onion and celery. Cook without browning until onion is transparent. Add bean sprouts and their liquid. Keep hot.
5. Reduce pressure in pressure pan and remove lid. Mix arrowroot with a little water and stir in. Cook until thickened. Tip in the vegetables. Add more salt if necessary and pepper. Serve with the rice.

BRAISED BEEF, LAZY WAY

Times: 20 minutes for bladebone *Serves 6*
25 minutes for cheaper stewing steak

In this recipe preparation time as well as cooking time is saved, especially if you get your butcher to trim and cut the meat into cubes for you. An excellent dish if you are arriving home at the same time as family or guests.

1½–2 lb (¾–1 kg) stewing steak
3 lamb kidneys (optional)
2 level tablespoons flour
1 teaspoon margarine
2 medium-sized onions, peeled and chopped, or 2 tablespoons dried
½ pint (250 ml) stock, or water with 1 beef stock cube
½ teaspoon thyme
salt and pepper to taste
carrots, celery, mushrooms, etc. (*optional*, see step 3)

1. The steak should be trimmed and cut into neat cubes and the kidneys skinned and quartered, with the core and fatty pieces removed. Toss all the meat in the flour.
2. Melt the margarine in the pressure pan, then add the onions and meat and cook them in the fat for 1 minute.
3. Add the liquid, thyme and seasoning and mix well. At this stage any other vegetables can be added, provided the pan is not more than two-thirds full of liquid. *See p. 24*, 'Adding whole vegetables'.
4. Fix lid and bring to pressure. *Allow times given above.*
5. Reduce pressure and remove lid. Check gravy for seasoning.

BEEF BRAISE WITH BACON AND MUSHROOMS

Times: 20 minutes for bladebone *Serves 4*
25 minutes for cheaper stewing steak

Here the beef is cut into serving-sized pieces about 3 in × 4 in. A dish worthy of both family and guests.

4 rashers streaky bacon
about 1½ lb (¾ kg) stewing steak
2 medium-sized onions, peeled and chopped
4 oz (100 g) mushrooms, washed and sliced
1½ level tablespoons flour
½ pint (¼ litre) stock, or water with beef stock cube
½ teaspoon dried mixed herbs or thyme
salt and pepper to taste

1. Remove rinds and cut bacon into 1 in pieces and drop into pressure pan. Begin to fry.
2. Trim fat if necessary from the meat and cut into pieces about 3 in × 4 in. When fat has run out from bacon, fry the meat, two or three pieces at a time, until lightly browned. Remove them to a plate.
3. Add onions and mushrooms to pressure pan and cook together for 2 minutes. Add flour and toss around until blended.
4. Add liquid, herbs and seasoning. Stir well. Put the meat back.
5. Fix lid and bring to pressure. *Allow times shown above.*
6. Reduce pressure and remove lid. Check gravy for seasoning.

Beef braise with wine: Use half red wine and half stock in step 4, or all wine may be used.

Beef braise with tomatoes: Use a small can of Italian peeled tomatoes and make up to ½ pint (¼ litre) with water. Add 2 teaspoons brown sugar. For extra piquancy, add 2 teaspoons of Worcester sauce.

Beef braise with beer: Use ½ pint (¼ litre) dark beer instead of the water. Add the stock cube.

BRAISED STEAKS SUPREME

Time: 22–25 minutes (see step 6) *Serves 4*

This is a dish for the gourmet. The steaks are marinated in a mixture of wine, onion, bay leaf and garlic, then covered with a delicious mixture of onions, mushrooms and bacon, and cooked on the rack above a rich dark gravy.

4 slices of bladebone steak, each approximately ¾ in thick and weighing about 6 oz (150 g)
2 rashers streaky bacon
8 oz (¼ kg) peeled and finely chopped onions
4 oz (100 g) mushrooms, washed and sliced
salt and pepper to taste
1 tablespoon butter or other fat
1½ tablespoons flour
¼ pint (125 ml) water
1 beef stock cube or 3 teaspoons soy sauce
parsley

MARINADE: *¼ pint (125 ml) red wine, 4 tablespoons water, 1 quartered onion, 1 bay leaf, and 1 peeled clove of garlic*

1. Trim the steaks, put them into a dish with the marinade. Allow to stand for several hours, turning twice.
2. Remove rinds and cut the bacon into ½ in pieces with scissors. Drop into pressure pan and begin to fry. Add the onions, mushrooms and a little salt and pepper. Fry together for 5 minutes. Lift this mixture out and put on a plate.
3. Heat the fat in the pressure pan. Dust the steaks with the flour and fry for a few minutes on either side. Lift out and arrange on trivet or rack. Pile the fried mixture on top.
4. Add cube or soy sauce to water and pour in. Add marinade liquid. Cut marinated onion into smaller pieces and add. Season with salt and pepper, and add the garlic, crushed.
5. Lift the rack and meat by putting the end of a large pointed spoon into one of the slits. Lower into pressure pan.
6. Fix lid and bring to pressure. *Allow 22 minutes.* If meat is 1 in thick, allow 25 minutes.
7. Reduce pressure and remove lid. Lift out the meat on the rack. Arrange steaks on a heated serving dish and serve gravy separately. Garnish with parsley.

COMPANY STEW WITH NOODLES

Time: 25 minutes *Serves 6*

A rather special sort of stew. Ideal for an after-theatre supper on a wintry night. It could be made the day before and reheated just before it is needed. The pressure pan will then be free to cook the noodles.

1 lb (½ kg) stewing steak
½ lb (¼ kg) pork fillet
2 veal kidneys, or ½ lb (¼ kg) sheep or ox
2 tablespoons oil or butter
2 level tablespoons flour
3 onions, peeled and chopped
4 oz (100 g) mushrooms, washed and halved
1 small can of mushroom soup (¼ pint, 125 ml)
¼ pint (125 ml) white wine (or a substitute of 1 tablespoon vinegar, 1 tablespoon sugar and a bare ¼ pint water)
½ teaspoon thyme or bouquet garni
salt and pepper to taste
1 clove of garlic, crushed (optional)
6 oz (150 g) noodles

1. Trim the steak and cut both steak and pork into 1 in cubes. Trim fat and skin from kidneys and cut into slices.
2. Heat fat in pressure pan. Add meat and fry until seared.
3. Add flour and onions and continue frying for 2 minutes. Remove from heat.
4. Add the mushrooms, soup, wine (or substitute), and herbs and seasoning, including garlic if liked. Stir well together and return to heat.
5. Fix lid and bring to pressure. *Allow 25 minutes.*
6. Reduce pressure and remove lid. Check for seasoning.
7. Cook the noodles in another pan, or tip the stew into a casserole and cook the noodles in the washed pressure pan (*see p. 197*). Serve with the stew.

BEEF CURRY AND RICE

Time: 25 minutes *Serves 6*

Many a host will choose this dish as a party piece, knowing it is easy to prepare, reliable and allows scope for the cook's own individuality.

1 level tablespoon butter, margarine or oil
2 lb (1 kg) stewing steak
1½ level tablespoons flour
1 or more level tablespoons curry powder
2 onions, peeled and chopped (any size)
2 eating apples, peeled and sliced
4 oz (100 g or ½ cup) sultanas
2 tablespoons tart jam
1 level tablespoon brown sugar
2 teaspoons soy sauce (or 1 beef stock cube)
¼ pint (125 ml) water
salt and pepper to taste
1 or 2 cloves of garlic, crushed
1 lb (½ kg) long-grain rice
accompaniments (see step 7)

1. Melt fat in pressure pan.
2. Trim the steak, cut it into 1 in cubes and add. Fry for a minute, then add flour, curry powder and onions. Fry together for about 5 minutes until browned. Remove from heat.
3. Add apples, sultanas, jam, sugar, soy sauce, water, seasoning and garlic. Mix well.
4. Return to heat and fix lid. Bring to pressure. *Allow 25 minutes.*
5. Reduce pressure and remove lid. Taste and add more salt if necessary.
6. Meantime, the rice can be cooking in another pan in 4 pints (2 litres) of boiling water and 2 level teaspoons salt. Boil rapidly, uncovered, for 5 minutes, then turn off heat, put on the lid and allow the rice to swell further for about 10 minutes.
7. Accompaniments should be served separately; for instance, little dishes of coconut (grated fresh or desiccated), chutney, salted peanuts, chopped gherkins and chopped green pepper.

CHILLI CON CARNE

Time: 10 minutes *Serves 4–5*

In South America this is a traditional dish, but many other countries include it in their culinary repertoire. The 'Chilli with Meat' is made with minced or chopped beef, flavoured with chilli powder and often extended with dried beans, notably red kidney or chilli beans.

1 level tablespoon margarine, butter, or oil
2 medium-sized onions, peeled and chopped

1 level tablespoon flour
1 lb (½ kg) minced beef
¼ pint (125 ml) stock, or water with 1 beef stock cube
2 rounded teaspoons chilli powder, or more to taste
2 rounded teaspoons brown sugar
salt and pepper to taste (2 teaspoons soy sauce may replace some of the salt)
15 oz (375 g) can of red kidney beans in sauce (see Note)

1. Heat fat in pressure pan and add onions. Fry gently for about 3 minutes.
2. Add mince and flour and continue to fry for another 3 minutes, moving around with a wooden spoon.
3. Add stock, chilli powder, sugar, seasoning and can of beans.
4. Stir together then fix lid and bring to pressure. *Allow 10 minutes.*
5. Reduce pressure and remove lid. Taste and add more seasoning if necessary.

Note: A can of baked beans in tomato sauce may replace the kidney beans. Reduce flour to 1 rounded teaspoon.

STEAK AND KIDNEY PIE

Times: 15 minutes pressure cooking
¾ hour in the oven
Serves 6

In spite of calorie counts and diet taboos, Steak and Kidney Pie is entrenched in the diet of the British, wherever in the world they may be. The pressure pan plays its part in saving over an hour's cooking time in the preparation of the meat and gravy. Shin beef is an excellent choice of meat for this dish.

1½ lb (¾ kg) stewing steak or shin beef
3 lamb kidneys, or 6 oz (150 g) ox kidney
1½ level tablespoons butter or other fat
2 onions, peeled and chopped
1½ level tablespoons flour
4 oz (100 g) mushrooms, washed and sliced
½ pint (¼ litre) stock, or water with 1 beef stock cube
½ teaspoon thyme
salt and pepper to taste (2 teaspoons soy sauce may replace some of the salt)
about ¾ lb (300 g) short or puff pastry

1. Trim fat and gristle from the meat and cut it into 1 in cubes. Remove fat, skin and core from kidneys and cut into pieces.
2. Heat fat in pressure pan. Add onions and fry for 2 minutes, then add the meats and fry for another 2 minutes. Add the flour and mix in. Remove from heat.
3. Add mushrooms, liquid, herbs and seasoning. Stir everything together and return to heat.
4. Fix lid and bring to pressure. *Allow 15 minutes.*
5. Reduce pressure and remove lid. Check gravy for seasoning then tip everything into a deep pie dish. Put in pie funnel. Preheat oven to 350 °F or mark 4.
6. Roll out the pastry. Wet the edge of the pie dish and put a 1 in strip of pastry around. Wet the strip then cover pie dish with the pastry. Make a hole in the centre to allow an escape of steam. Pastry leaves may be arranged around it. To give an attractive finish, brush the pastry with beaten egg.
7. Bake for about ¾ hour, or until browned.

STEAK AND KIDNEY PUDDING

Times: 20 minutes without pressure and 1½ hours at pressure — *Serves 4*

In an ordinary saucepan this old-established family meat dish would need 4 hours. Pressure-cooked it will emerge brown and succulent in under two.

Suet Crust (see Farmhouse Apple Pudding, p. 162)
¾ lb (300 g) stewing steak
¼ lb (100 g) kidney, lamb or ox
1 medium-sized onion, peeled and chopped
1 level teaspoon salt and a little pepper
¼ pint (125 ml) water
1 beef stock cube
½ teaspoon thyme

1. Make the suet crust and cut off ¼ of it for the lid. Roll out to ⅛ in thickness.
2. Line a 2 pint (1 litre) pudding bowl with the crust and trim.
3. Cut the meat into 1 in cubes and add to bowl. Skin, core and trim fatty bits from kidneys, cut into pieces and mix in with the meat. Add the onion.

4. Add the cube, seasoning and thyme to the water and pour over the meat etc.
5. Roll out the lid and fit over the bowl. Pinch firmly with the lining, making sure that no gravy can escape.
6. Pour 1½ pints (¾ litre) water into pressure pan and insert rack. Begin to heat.
7. Cover bowl with foil, making sure there are no little holes or tears, and secure tightly with string or a rubber band. Lower into pressure pan and fix lid.
8. Let the water boil and cook without pressure for 20 minutes. Now close vent and bring to pressure. *Allow 1½ hours.*
9. Move pan to a cool surface and let the pressure reduce gradually. Remove lid. Lift out pudding and take off the foil. Serve from the bowl.

BOEUF MARINÉ

Time: 1 hour *Serves about 6*

As with the Braised Steaks Supreme (*p. 92*) the meat for this dish is first impregnated with a marinade mixture. The circumference is then wrapped in bacon and later, after cooking, it is given an unusual garnish.

2½ lb (1¼ kg) topside steak in one piece about 3 in thick
1 rounded tablespoon butter or margarine or 2 tablespoons oil
2 level tablespoons flour
2 leeks, washed and cut into 1 in pieces
½ pint (¼ litre) stock, or water with 1 beef stock cube
½ teaspoon thyme
3 celery stalks, chopped
salt and pepper to taste
3 bacon rashers

MARINADE
2 tablespoons olive oil
1 sliced onion
¼ pint (125 ml) white wine
2 cloves
1 bay leaf
½ teaspoon salt
1 crushed clove of garlic

1. Mix ingredients for the marinade. Trim the meat, put it into the marinade and allow to stand for several hours or overnight, turning the meat twice.

D

2. Melt the butter, margarine or oil in the pressure pan. Lift the meat from the marinade, drain well then coat on both sides with the flour. Fry on both sides until browned. Lift out and put on to a plate.
3. Add the rest of the flour to the pan and stir into the remaining fat, then add the leeks, stock, marinade liquid, herbs, celery and seasoning. Stir all together and return to heat.
4. Insert rack. Wrap bacon rashers, rinds removed, around the circumference of the meat and tie with string. Place meat on rack.
5. Fix lid and bring to pressure. *Allow 1 hour.*
6. Reduce pressure and remove lid. Lift out the meat. Remove string and put a stuffed olive on to the end of several cocktail picks and push into bacon around the meat, about 1½ in apart.

POT-ROAST OF TOPSIDE or FRESH BRISKET

Times: 50 minutes for a 2 lb (1 kg) piece
1 hour for a 2½ lb (1¼ kg) piece
1¼ hours for a 3 lb (1½ kg) piece

Serves up to 8, depending on size

Both these cuts are at their best when pot-roasted, and pressure-cooking is ideal for the purpose. The beef will cook in half the usual time and will emerge succulent, tender and impregnated with the flavour of herbs and vegetables.

a thick piece of topside or boned rolled fresh brisket, no more than 3 lb (1½ kg) in weight
2 level tablespoons flour
1 pint (½ litre) water
1 tablespoon fat
1 tablespoon vinegar and 1 teaspoon sugar
a bay leaf or a teaspoon of thyme, basil or tarragon
2 teaspoons salt and a little pepper
1 or 2 cloves of garlic, crushed (optional)
small whole vegetables such as onions, carrots, parsnips and potatoes, peeled
soy sauce or gravy browning

1. Dust the meat all over with the flour. Melt fat in pressure pan and when very hot fry the meat until browned. Tip away any surplus fat. Insert rack or trivet and put meat on to it.
2. Add water, vinegar and sugar, herb and seasoning, including garlic if liked.

3. Fix lid and bring to pressure. *Allow 15 minutes less than time shown above*, then reduce pressure and remove lid.
4. Put in the whole peeled vegetables. Do not fill the pan more than two-thirds with liquid, *see p. 24*. Fix the lid and bring again to pressure. *Allow the final 15 minutes.*
5. Reduce pressure and remove lid. Remove rack and meat. To reduce fat from gravy, tip it into a tall jug, leave for a few minutes then spoon off the fat that will rise to the top. Use some of this broth for gravy, adding a little gravy browning. Use the rest for soup.

SALT (OR CORNED) BEEF WITH MUSTARD SAUCE

Times: 55 minutes for a 2 lb (1 kg) piece
1 hour and 5 minutes for a 2½ lb (1¼ kg) piece
1½ hours for a 3 lb (1½ kg) piece

Serves up to 8, depending on size

The meat may be served hot with vegetables and Mustard Sauce (*p. 192*), or cold with a salad. Delicious when pressed.

2–3 lb (1–1½ kg) salt brisket or silverside
water to cover
1 tablespoon vinegar
4 cloves
1 bay leaf
1 onion, peeled and halved
2 teaspoons sugar
whole carrots, onions and parsnips or potatoes, peeled

1. Place the meat on the rack in the pressure cooker. Cover it with cold water. Bring to the boil, then throw away the water to get rid of excess salt.
2. Add 1 pint (½ litre) fresh water, also the vinegar, cloves, bay leaf, onion and sugar. Fix lid and bring to pressure.
3. *Allow all but 15 minutes of times given above.*
4. Reduce pressure and remove lid. Add the whole vegetables. Do not fill the pan more than two-thirds with liquid, *see p. 24*. Fix lid again and bring to pressure. *Allow the 15 minutes.*
5. Meanwhile make the Mustard Sauce.
6. Reduce pressure and remove lid. Lift out the meat. Serve hot with the vegetables and sauce, or cold with a salad.

See also **Pot-au-feu** *on p. 50.*

GALANTINE OF BEEF AND HAM

Time: 25 minutes *Serves 5–6*

A summertime mould that will set firm with the aspic in the bones. It will cut into meaty slices for a cold meal and is good for a picnic.

1 ham bone, preferably with about ¼ lb (100 g) of ham on it. If it hasn't, buy a good ¼ lb of ham in addition
1½ lb (¾ kg) shin meat and a piece of shin bone about 1 lb (½ kg) in weight
½ pint (¼ litre) water
1 medium-sized onion, peeled and chopped, or 1 tablespoon dried
1 bay leaf
1 teaspoon each of celery and ordinary salt and a little pepper
garlic (optional)

1. Trim away fat and gristle, cut the meat into 1 in cubes and put into pressure pan. If you have bought the ham separately, cut it into pieces and add.
2. Add all the bones, the water, onion, bay leaf and seasoning. Fix lid and bring to pressure. *Allow 25 minutes.*
3. Reduce pressure and remove lid. Lift out the bones and bay leaf. When cool enough to handle, cut away any meat clinging to the bones. Cut it up and add to pressure pan.
4. Have ready a 1½ pint (¾ litre) dish and spoon the meat into it.
5. Boil up the broth for a few minutes, then pour about ½ pint (¼ litre) of it over the meat. (Use the remaining broth later to enrich a soup.)
6. Put galantine in refrigerator until firm. Remove fat from the top. Dip bowl for a few seconds into hot water, then turn out. Surround with lettuce, hard-boiled eggs and salad vegetables.

Galantine of veal and ham: Use stewing veal and a knuckle of veal, instead of the beef and shin bone. *Allow 20 minutes.*

STUFFED RUMP STEAK

Time: 35 minutes *Serves 4–6*

This is a meat-stretching and succulent way to cook rump steak. It is bought in one thick piece, stuffed with a savoury stuffing, and then browned and pot-roasted in a delicious gravy.

1½–2 lb (¾–1 kg) rump steak in one piece 2 in thick
2½ oz (62 g or 1¼ cups) fresh breadcrumbs
½ teaspoon thyme or mixed herbs
1 medium-sized onion, peeled and grated
1 tablespoon parsley, chopped
2 teaspoons butter or margarine
½ teaspoon salt and a little pepper
2 tablespoons fat

GRAVY

2 onions, peeled, chopped
1 level tablespoon flour
½ pint (¼ litre) stock, or water with 1 beef stock cube (or half water half wine may be used)
salt and pepper to taste
1 clove of garlic, crushed (optional)

1. Ask the butcher to cut a pocket in the steak ready for stuffing.
2. Make the stuffing by mixing together the breadcrumbs, herbs, onion, parsley and seasoning. Chop in the butter or margarine.
3. Trim any surplus fat from the steak. Stuff the steak, then secure with string or small skewers.
4. Melt the fat in the pressure pan and when very hot, fry the steak on all sides until browned. Lift out on to a plate.
5. Leave a little fat in the pan and add the onions. Fry for 2 minutes, then add the flour and continue cooking for another 2 minutes. Remove from heat.
6. Stir in the liquid and seasoning. Add garlic if liked. Stir well and return to heat. Cook until gravy has just thickened, then insert rack or trivet. Put the meat on it.
7. Fix lid and bring to pressure. *Allow 35 minutes.* The extra time is needed because the meat is in one piece.
8. Reduce pressure and remove lid. Remove string or skewers from meat. Taste gravy and add more seasoning if necessary.

OX-TONGUE

Time: 1 hour — *Serves 6–10 depending on size*

Because of its long shape the 3 lb limit can be exceeded with tongue. The heat will penetrate satisfactorily.

When the Family Bible was one of the heaviest weights in the house, it was often called upon to play a role for which it was not really designed, namely to press the cooked tongue. Today the Family Bible has shrunk with the size of the family and we have to seek other heavy weights.

1 4 lb (2 kg) ox-tongue
water
1 tablespoon vinegar
4 cloves
2 teaspoons sugar
1 bay leaf

1. Wash the tongue well in cold water.
2. Place tongue on rack in pressure pan and pour in 2 pints (1 litre) of water. Cover with a plate and bring slowly to the boil. Boil gently for 10 minutes, then throw away the water.
3. Add 2 pints (1 litre) fresh water, and the vinegar, cloves, sugar and bay leaf. Fix lid and bring to pressure. *Allow 1 hour.*
4. Reduce pressure and remove lid. Lift out tongue and remove skin.
5. If it is to be served cold put it into a bowl, cover with small saucer or plate and press with heavy weights. Leave to press for several hours, or preferably overnight.
6. If it is to be served hot, either serve whole with a sauce or cut into slices and arrange on a hot dish, again serving with a sauce. The Cumberland Sauce (*p. 194*) is ideal.

Calves' tongues: 45 minutes. Serve with a sauce (*pp. 192–4*).

Lambs' tongues: 20–25 minutes. Serve with a sauce (*pp. 192–4*).

OXTAIL, BRAISED

Total time: 55 minutes *Serves 4*

As I have mentioned before, a pressure pan is ideal for anything that is small and tough. An oxtail, when disjointed, comes into both these categories. The gravy becomes very fatty while cooking, so it is usual to make the dish in two parts. In this way all the excess fat may be easily removed.

about 3–3½ lb (1½–1¾ kg) oxtail
3 level tablespoons flour
3 tablespoons oil, butter or margarine
2 pints (1 litre) water
3 teaspoons salt and a little pepper
½ bay leaf and a little thyme
1 tablespoon vinegar

2 rounded teaspoons brown sugar
4 or more whole onions, peeled
4 or more whole carrots, peeled
whole potatoes (optional)
2 teaspoons soy sauce, or 1 beef stock cube

First cooking

1. Disjoint the oxtail (or buy already disjointed). Roll in flour, using it all.
2. Heat fat in pressure pan and when hot, fry the joints until lightly browned. Remove them to a plate.
3. Add water, seasoning, herbs, vinegar and sugar. Stir, then put the joints back.
4. Fix lid and bring to pressure. *Allow 40 minutes.*
5. Reduce pressure and remove lid. Pour broth off into a bowl and set aside until cold. Put oxtail into another bowl or on to a plate.

Second cooking

1. Lift fat from broth and pour half of the broth back into pressure pan. The rest can be used as the basis for a soup. Add oxtail and the whole vegetables and the soy sauce or stock cube.
2. Fix lid and again bring to pressure. *Allow another 15 minutes.*
3. Reduce pressure and remove lid. Check gravy for seasoning.

MEAT BALLS IN GRAVY

Time: 10 minutes *Serves 6*

All continental countries have their traditional meat balls. The recipes vary from country to country, but basically the ingredients are those given here. The English have their rissoles and if Mrs. Beeton's recipe is the criterion, it is the most economical of all. She puts in ¾ lb of breadcrumbs to 1 lb of meat, a proportion that would be scorned today!

1½ lb (¾ kg) minced beef
1 or 2 onions, peeled, and grated or finely chopped
3 oz (75 g or 1½ cups) soft breadcrumbs
1 tablespoon parsley, chopped
½ teaspoon thyme
1 beaten egg
1½ teaspoons salt, and a little pepper
flour
2 tablespoons margarine or oil

GRAVY (see steps 3 and 4)

1 level tablespoon flour
½ pint (¼ litre) water
½ lb (¼ kg) peeled tomatoes or ¼ pint (125 ml) red wine
salt and pepper
2 teaspoons sugar

1. Combine the beef, onions, breadcrumbs, parsley, thyme, seasoning and beaten egg. With floury hands, form into balls, about 2–2½ in in diameter.
2. Melt half the fat in the pressure pan. When hot, fry the meat balls until lightly browned all over. Remove to a plate.
3. Add remaining fat to the pan, then add 1 level tablespoon flour and cook for 2 minutes. Remove from heat.
4. Add water and tomatoes or wine. Return to heat and stir and cook until just boiling. Add 1 level teaspoon salt, a little pepper and 2 teaspoons sugar. Insert rack.
5. Put the meat balls on the rack. Fix lid and bring to pressure. *Allow 10 minutes.*
6. Reduce pressure and remove lid. Taste gravy and add more seasoning if necessary.

SWEET-SOUR MEAT BALLS

Time: 10 minutes *Serves 4*

These might appear to be Chinese, but they are really Swedish. The main ingredients for the balls are meat and rice and the gravy has an exotic sweet-sour flavour.

1 lb (½ kg) minced beef
¼ lb (100 g) minced or finely chopped ham or bacon
6 oz (150 g or 1 cup) cooked rice
1 medium onion, peeled and grated
1 tablespoon chopped parsley
½ teaspoon thyme
1 teaspoon salt and a little pepper
1 egg beaten with 2 tablespoons water
2 tablespoons oil or other fat for frying

GRAVY

1 tablespoon margarine
1 level dessertspoon flour
1 chopped onion, any size
½ pint (¼ litre) water
4 tablespoons vinegar
2 rounded tablespoons brown sugar
1 clove of garlic, crushed
salt and pepper to taste (2 teaspoons soy sauce may replace some of the salt)

1. Combine all the ingredients (except the oil) for the meat balls. With floury hands form into balls about 2½ in in diameter.
2. Melt the oil or fat in the pressure pan. Fry the meat balls until lightly browned. Lift on to a plate.
3. Melt the margarine in the pressure pan and add the flour and onions. Fry together for about 2 minutes. Remove from heat.
4. Add the water, vinegar, brown sugar, garlic and seasoning. Stir together then return to heat.
5. Replace the meat balls. Fix lid and bring to pressure. *Allow 10 minutes.*
6. Reduce pressure and remove lid. Taste gravy and add more seasoning if necessary.

MEAT LOAF

Time: 30 minutes *Serves 4–5*

If the oblong shape of the usual meat loaf pan won't fit into your pressure saucepan, use a square or round metal cake tin, about 6–7 in across and 2½–3 in deep. The loaf may be eaten hot or cold. Perfect for a picnic.

1 lb (½ kg) minced beef
3 oz (75 g) stale bread with crusts and ½ cup boiling water
1 onion (about 6 oz, 150 g), grated or minced
½ teaspoon thyme
1 standard egg, beaten
1 rounded teaspoon salt and a little pepper
1 tablespoon chopped parsley
2 or 3 streaky bacon rashers

1. Roughly break up the bread and put with the boiling water into a small bowl. Allow to soak while preparing the rest of the loaf.
2. Tip meat into a mixing bowl and add the onion, herb, beaten egg, seasoning and parsley.
3. Put rack into pressure pan and pour in 1 pint (½ litre) water. Begin to heat.
4. Mash the bread until smooth, tip off surplus water, and add bread to meat etc. Stir well.
5. Remove rinds from rashers and arrange bacon on bottom of tin. Put meat mixture on top and press well down. Cover with foil and secure with string. Lower into pressure pan.

6. Fix lid and bring to pressure. *Allow 30 minutes.*
7. Reduce pressure and remove lid. Lift out loaf and pour off the liquid into a cup. Use for gravy or soup. Turn loaf out.

Meat loaf with sausage meat added: To main recipe add ½ lb (¼ kg) mashed sausage meat. Will increase servings to 6.

Meat loaf with rice: Follow main recipe, but replace bread and water with 1½ cups cooked rice.

MINCE AND RICE QUICKIE

Time: 8 minutes *Serves 5–6*

A recipe that is economical and nourishing as well as speedy. The rice, onions, meat and flavourings are all cooked together and the final dish provides generous helpings with only 1 lb of meat.

1 lb (½ kg) minced beef
6 oz (150 g or 6 rounded tablespoons) uncooked rice
1 pint (½ litre) water
1 large or 2 smaller onions, peeled and sliced thinly
½ teaspoon thyme
1 beef stock cube or 2 teaspoons soy sauce
2 teaspoons tomato purée
2 teaspoons brown sugar
2 teaspoons Worcester sauce
salt and pepper to taste

1. Put all the ingredients into the pressure pan. Mix together.
2. Fix lid and bring to pressure. *Allow 8 minutes.*
3. Reduce pressure and remove lid. Taste and add more seasoning if necessary.

This could be tipped into a serving dish, topped with grated cheese and put under the grill or into the oven until the cheese has melted and browned slightly.

Curried Mince and Rice: Add 3 or more teaspoons curry powder, 1 level tablespoon sugar and a few sultanas.

MINCE AND DUMPLINGS

Times: 8 minutes for mince plus 15 minutes without pressure with the dumplings — *Serves 4*

Not a recipe for slimmers, but appetising and nourishing for a hungry family.

2 teaspoons butter or other fat
1 lb (½ kg) minced beef
1 level tablespoon flour
½ lb (¼ kg) peeled sliced tomatoes, or a can of peeled Italian tomatoes (see step 2)
2 teaspoons brown sugar
2 medium-sized onions, peeled and chopped
¼ pint (125 ml) water
2 teaspoons Worcester sauce
salt and pepper to taste

DUMPLINGS

8 oz (¼ kg) self-raising flour
½ teaspoon baking powder
½ teaspoon salt
3 oz (75 g) suet
about ¼ pint (125 ml) water

1. Melt fat in pressure pan then add beef and flour. Fry until lightly browned.
2. Add the tomatoes, sugar, onions, water, Worcester sauce and seasoning. Stir well. ¼ pint (125 ml) extra water may replace tomatoes.
3. Fix lid and bring to pressure. *Allow 8 minutes.*
4. Meanwhile make the dumplings. Combine the flour, baking powder, salt and suet, then mix to a soft (slightly sticky) dough with the water. With floury hands form into balls about 2–2½ in diameter.
5. Reduce pressure and remove lid. Add 4 tablespoons water. Return pan to heat and bring mince to a gentle boil. Drop in the dumplings, cover pan with an enamel plate and boil for the 15 minutes, no longer. Serve at once while the dumplings are light and fluffy.

BRAISED VEAL (family recipe)

Time: 17 minutes *Serves 4–5*

With a reliable basic recipe, many other dishes may be created. Changes and additions are suggested at the end of the recipe.

about 1–1½ lb (½–¾ kg) veal, either stewing, fillet or chops
2 or 3 streaky bacon rashers
2 medium-sized onions, peeled and chopped
2 level tablespoons flour
½ pint stock, or water with a chicken or veal stock cube
½ teaspoon thyme or rosemary
1 clove garlic (optional)
salt and pepper to taste
for additions, see below

1. The veal should be about ¾–1 in thick. Cut stewing or fillet veal into 1½ in pieces. Trim chops.
2. Remove rinds from bacon. Cut bacon into 2 in pieces and drop into pressure pan. Begin to fry.
3. Add onions and continue frying until fat runs out.
4. Add meat and fry for 2 minutes, then sprinkle in the flour and fry for another 2 minutes. Remove from heat.
5. Add liquid, herbs, garlic if liked, seasoning, and any of the extra vegetables suggested below. Whole potatoes may be arranged on top, or be put into divider. Sprinkle with salt.
6. Fix lid and bring to pressure. *Allow 17 minutes.*
7. Reduce pressure and remove lid. Check seasoning.

Additions: May include ¼ lb mushrooms, 2 or 3 scraped sliced carrots, 4 or 5 sticks of celery, washed and cut into 1 in pieces. Leeks could replace all or some of the onion.

Veal with tomatoes: Reduce stock to ¼ pint (125 ml) and add ½ lb peeled sliced tomatoes or 1 small can of peeled tomatoes with liquid. Add 2 teaspoons sugar and use 1 teaspoon dried basil instead of the other herbs. (Pimentos may be used instead of tomatoes.)

Veal pie: Make any of the above recipes, but *allow 10 minutes instead of 17.* Tip into pie dish, insert pie funnel and cover with pastry in the usual way. Bake for 40 minutes or until a golden brown.

BLANQUETTE DE VEAU

Time: 17 minutes *Serves 4*

A *blanquette* is a stew with a cream sauce and mushrooms. The word might indicate that the recipe originated in France, but this is not so. The dish was known in England long before it became fashionable to call cooking 'cuisine'! It was a farmhouse dish originally known as 'Veal in Cream Gravy'.

1½ lb (¾ kg) either stewing veal or fillet of veal about ¾ in thick
1 level tablespoon flour
1 level tablespoon butter or margarine
¼ pint (125 ml) white wine (or water with 1 tablespoon lemon juice and 2 teaspoons sugar)
8 or more small whole onions, peeled
8 oz (200 g) white mushrooms, washed and halved (or use canned)
½ teaspoon thyme
salt and pepper to taste
1 clove of garlic, crushed (optional)
½ pint (¼ litre) Cream Sauce (p. 192) or single cream
1 tablespoon chopped parsley

1. Cut the veal into 2 in pieces, trim away any surplus fat and coat the pieces with the flour.
2. Melt the butter or margarine in the pressure pan. Add the veal and fry for 2 minutes. Remove from heat.
3. Add the wine (or substitute), the onions, mushrooms, thyme, seasoning and garlic if liked. Mix well.
4. Return to heat and fix lid. Bring to pressure. *Allow 17 minutes.* Make the Cream Sauce if using this.
5. Reduce pressure and remove lid.
6. Add the Cream Sauce or cream and the parsley. Check seasoning. Reheat before serving.

PARTY VEAL CASSEROLE

Time: 17 minutes *Serves 6*

Served with a large dish of rice and a salad or green vegetables (peas and beans for instance), this would be ideal for a dinner party or winter buffet supper.

4 oz (100 g) streaky bacon
2 lb (1 kg) stewing or pie veal or fillet of veal
1½ level tablespoons flour
2 teaspoons butter
1 large Spanish onion, peeled and chopped, or 2 smaller ones
2 rounded teaspoons sugar
7 oz (175 g) jar of stuffed olives
¼ pint (125 ml) white wine
¼ pint (125 ml) stock, or water with 1 veal or chicken stock cube
salt and pepper to taste
½ lb (200 g) button mushrooms, washed
1 clove of garlic, crushed (optional)
3–4 tablespoons double cream

1. Remove rinds and cut bacon into 1½ in pieces. Fry gently in pressure pan for 2 or 3 minutes.
2. Cut veal into 1½ in pieces, trim away any surplus fat, and coat with the flour. Add to bacon in pan, also add butter, and cook for 2 minutes. Add onions and toss around. Remove from heat.
3. Add sugar, wine, stock, seasoning, mushrooms and garlic if liked. Add 1 tablespoon of the liquor from the jar of stuffed olives.
4. Fix lid and bring to pressure. *Allow 17 minutes.*
5. Reduce pressure and remove lid.
6. Cut olives in halves and add. Add the cream. Taste gravy and add more salt and pepper if necessary.

Variations: ½ lb (¼ kg) peeled tomatoes may replace ¼ pint (125 ml) of the water. Soured cream may replace the fresh. 3–4 sticks of celery may be added. 1 large or 2 smaller leeks could replace the onions. A bay leaf or ½ teaspoon thyme or mixed herbs may be added.

STUFFED VEAL DOMINICAINE

Times: 45 minutes for a 2 lb (1 kg) piece
50 minutes for a 2½ lb (1¼ kg) piece
1¼ hours for a 3 lb (1½ kg) piece

Serves 4–8

It is the special stuffing that gives this veal dish its name. Rice is combined with liver pâté, mushrooms, onion, herbs and truffles. The meat is browned well first, then steam-roasted until tender.

a piece of the thick end of the leg of veal, see weights above
2 tablespoons margarine or oil
a little flour
1 pint (½ litre) water
1 onion, peeled and halved
1 teaspoon salt

STUFFING
12 oz (300 g or 1½ cups) cooked rice (p. 198)
4 oz (100 g) chopped liver pâté
1 tablespoon chopped parsley
½ teaspoon thyme
4 oz (100 g) white mushrooms washed, sliced and fried in a little butter
1 dessertspoon chopped truffle (optional)
½ teaspoon salt and a little pepper
1 tablespoon softened butter

1. Ask the butcher to cut a good pocket in the veal.
2. For the stuffing, combine in a bowl, the rice, pâté, herbs, mushrooms, truffle if liked, seasoning and softened butter. Mix well.
3. Push this stuffing into the cavity and secure with thread or tiny skewers.
4. Melt fat in pressure pan. Dust veal lightly with flour, then fry until browned all over. If any fat remains, tip it away.
5. Lift meat out and put rack into pan. Place meat on it, then add water, onion and salt.
6. Fix lid and bring to pressure. *Allow times as given above.*
7. Reduce pressure and remove lid.

Note: Other vegetables, such as celery, leeks, carrots and parsnips, could be added besides the onion.

VEAL AND HAM ROLLS

Time: 15 minutes *Serves 4*

The veal is beaten out by the butcher to ⅛ in thickness, cut into slices and rolled up with ham. For a special occasion the rolls could be served with fruit. Pears or peaches with stoned prunes or cherries in the hollows would look attractive.

4 oz (100 g) thinly sliced ham
1¼ lb (600 g) fillet of veal cut into 8 slices and beaten out to ⅛ in thickness
a little French mustard
1 tablespoon oil or butter
2 onions, peeled and chopped
½ pint (¼ litre) stock or water with 1 veal stock cube, or all or part white wine may be used

½ teaspoon mixed herbs
salt and pepper to taste (2 teaspoons soy sauce may replace some of the salt)
1 level tablespoon flour
white button mushrooms, washed (optional)
chopped parsley

1. Cut ham into 8 pieces and place one on each slice of veal. Spread with a little French mustard. Roll up and secure with tiny skewers or thread.
2. Heat fat in pressure pan and fry rolls until seared. Remove them to a plate.
3. Add onions and flour and cook together for 2 minutes.
4. Add the liquid, herbs and seasoning. If liked add the mushrooms. Mix well, and add the rolls.
5. Fix lid and bring to pressure. *Allow 15 minutes.*
6. Reduce pressure and remove lid. Check seasoning.

To serve: Remove thread or skewers from rolls and place on heated serving dish. Pour gravy over. Surround if liked with pear or peach halves, their centres filled with stoned prunes or cherries. Sprinkle with chopped parsley.

BOILED LAMB OR MUTTON

Times: 25 minutes to the 1 lb (½ kg) for lamb
30 minutes to the 1 lb (½ kg) for mutton
Serves 5–6

'Mutton' is a word so seldom used nowadays, that one feels that it is in danger of disappearing completely from the language. Perhaps the phrase 'mutton dressed up as lamb' will mystify the generations ahead and send them rushing to the *Encyclopaedia Britannica.* There they will find that it is meat from an animal that has been walking the fields for years and so toughened its muscles.

about 3 lb (1½ kg) leg of lamb or mutton (larger than that is not suitable for pressure-cooking)
1 pint (½ litre) water
1 onion, peeled and halved
1 bay leaf
2 teaspoons salt and a little pepper
a few parsley stalks
vegetables (optional, see step 4)

1. Place rack in pressure pan and place meat on it.
2. Add the water, onion, bay leaf, salt, pepper and parsley stalks.
3. Fix lid and bring to pressure. *Allow times given for lamb or mutton, or 15 minutes less if vegetables are to be added.*
4. Whole potatoes, carrots, parsnips and onions may be added 15 minutes before the time is up. Reduce the pressure, remove the lid, add the vegetables; *see p. 24, 'Adding whole vegetables'*. Fix lid again, bring to pressure and *allow the extra time.*
5. Serve with Caper Sauce, Onion and Parsley Sauce, or Celery Sauce (*pp. 192, 193*).
6. Pour the broth into a bowl and put on one side until the fat has hardened. Remove it and use broth as a basis for soup.

LAMB JOINT JARDINIÈRE

Times: 25 minutes per lb (½ kg) for lamb
30 minutes per lb (½ kg) for mutton

Serves 5–6

A French lamb pot roast that will make a tender change from the oven roast.

- *1 level tablespoon butter or margarine*
- *1 large Spanish onion, or two small English ones, peeled and chopped*
- *1 small head of celery, or 6 sticks, trimmed and chopped*
- *a small leg or shoulder of lamb, no more than 3 lb (1½ kg)*
- *¾ pint (375 ml) water, or half water and half white wine may be used*
- *1 teaspoon tarragon*
- *1 good teaspoon salt and a little pepper*
- *2 level tablespoons flour*

1. Heat fat in pressure pan and add chopped onions and celery. Fry for 2 minutes.
2. Put in the meat and fry on all sides until seared. Remove to a plate.
3. To the vegetables in the pan add the liquid, herb and seasoning.
4. Put the trivet or rack into pressure pan and lower the meat on to it. Fix lid and bring to pressure. *Allow times shown above.*
5. Reduce pressure and remove lid. Lift out meat and keep warm. Strain the broth into a bowl and leave for a few minutes while the fat rises to the top.

6. Meanwhile mix the flour with a little cold water until smooth. Spoon the fat from the broth and pour the broth back into pressure pan. Thicken with the flour and water and boil for 3 minutes. Put the vegetables back. Serve the sauce and vegetables with the lamb.

SHOULDER OF LAMB, PLAIN JANE or GOURMET-STYLE

Time: 50–55 minutes, plus 15 minutes for roasting *Serves 4–6*

Either way a boned shoulder of lamb is a good buy for a braise-roast in your pressure pan. Here the meat is first pressure-cooked, then browned in the oven. Plain Jane will emerge browned and tender: gourmet-style will have more exotic trimmings.

2–2½ lb (1–1¼ kg) boned shoulder of lamb
stuffing if liked (see step 1)
3 tablespoons fat or 4 of oil
1 pint (½ litre) water
1 teaspoon salt and a little pepper
½ teaspoon rosemary or other herb
2 level tablespoons flour
(gourmet-style extras are indicated in the recipes which follow)

1. The butcher will bone the shoulder for you and tie it if you wish. If you intend to stuff it, untie, cut the cavity along further to hold more stuffing, and tie up again after pushing in the stuffing. Choose a stuffing from Chapter 7—not a rice stuffing for this dish.
2. Heat the fat or oil in the pressure pan and when very hot, brown the meat all over. Lift out and put on to a plate.
3. Tip out the surplus fat and save it. Add the water, salt and pepper and herb. Insert the rack or trivet and put the meat on it.
4. Fix lid and bring to pressure. *Allow 50–55 minutes.*
5. Reduce pressure and remove lid. Lift out the meat and put into an oven dish. Pour the broth into a bowl.
6. If the meat is pressure-cooked in the morning, the broth could be put away until cold, then the fat lifted off. If you are cooking the meat in time for dinner, let the broth stand in a tall slender jug while the meat is in the oven, then spoon the fat off.
7. Heat the oven to 350 °F or gas mark 4. Roast the meat for about 15 minutes in the surplus fat. Put the meat on to a heated dish,

pour off most of the fat and make gravy in the usual way, using about ¾ pint (375 ml) of the broth. Two or 3 teaspoons of soy sauce may be used to give extra colour and flavour to the gravy.

Shoulder of lamb with apricots and brandy: Drain the syrup from a 15½ oz (440 g) can of apricot-halves and use as part of the liquid in step 3. While the meat is cooking, soak the well-drained apricots in 2 or 3 tablespoons brandy, turning them once or twice. Heat through on a shallow ovenware dish. Just before serving, tip the syrupy brandy into the gravy and surround the meat with the apricots. To give extra colour, put a glacé or Maraschino cherry in the centre of each apricot. Garnish with parsley or watercress.

Shoulder of lamb with spiced peach or apricot sauce: Drain the syrup from a 15½ oz (440 g) can of apricots or peaches into a small saucepan. Add ½ teaspoon each of ginger, nutmeg and ground coriander (or cinnamon). Bring to the boil. Mash the fruit and tip into a sauceboat. Boil the spicy syrup for 5 minutes until a little thicker, then strain over the mashed fruit and mix in. 2 or 3 tablespoons of brandy or sherry may be added. Serve with the meat along with the gravy.

LAMB CHOPS WITH VEGETABLES

Time: 18 minutes (see step 5) *Serves 4*

No dividers or separator needed for this dish. Whole potatoes, whole onions and whole carrots are placed on top of the chops and everything will emerge perfectly cooked in 18 minutes.

4 chump or loin chops, ¾ in thick
1½ level tablespoons flour
1 level tablespoon butter, margarine or oil
½ pint (¼ litre) stock (or water with 1 chicken stock cube)
4 tablespoons white wine, or extra water
salt and pepper to taste (2 teaspoons soy sauce may replace some of the salt)
a little rosemary or mint
1 clove of garlic, crushed (optional)
whole peeled potatoes, onions and carrots (see step 4)

1. Trim some of the fat from the chops and snip the edges to prevent curling. Coat with the flour.
2. Melt the fat in the pressure pan. Fry chops, two at a time and put on to a plate. Tip away any surplus fat.
3. Add the liquid to the pan with the seasoning, herb and, if used, the garlic. Put the chops back.
4. Arrange the whole vegetables on top, *see p. 24, 'Adding whole vegetables'*, and sprinkle with salt.
5. Fix lid and bring to pressure. *Allow 18 minutes.* If the chops are only ½ in thick, *allow 14 minutes.*
6. Reduce pressure and remove lid. Check gravy for seasoning.

LAMB CHOPS, A QUICK WAY

Time: 18 minutes *Serves 4*

Prepare all ingredients as shown in the preceding recipe, except the flour. Melt the fat in the pan and add 1 heaped tablespoon packet soup, celery, mushroom, asparagus, vegetable or any flavour you wish. Cook for 2 minutes, then remove from heat. Add the chops, liquid, herb and seasoning. Arrange the whole vegetables on top, sprinkle them with salt, then proceed as in steps 5 and 6.

BRAISED LAMB CHOPS, ITALIAN STYLE

Time: 18 minutes *Serves 4*

Tomatoes, herbs, garlic (or mint) and sherry combine to give the Italian touch. Serve with a pasta (*see p. 197*).

4 or more lamb chops, chump, loin or the cheaper neck chops
1 tablespoon butter, oil or other fat
2 chopped onions, any size
1½ level tablespoons flour
½ lb (¼ kg) tomatoes, peeled and sliced, or 8 oz (¼ kg) can of Italian peeled tomatoes
1 teaspoon sugar
4 tablespoons sherry
4 tablespoons water
½ teaspoon basil
salt and pepper to taste
1 clove garlic, crushed, or 2 teaspoons chopped fresh mint
mushrooms (optional)

1. Trim some of the fat from the chops and snip the edges to prevent curling.
2. Heat the fat or oil in the pressure pan and fry the chops until lightly browned. Remove to a plate.
3. Add onions and fry for 2 minutes, then mix in the flour. Remove from heat and add the tomatoes, sugar, sherry, water, basil, seasoning and garlic if used. Add about 4 oz (100 g) mushrooms if liked. Mix well.
4. Return to heat and put in the chops. Sprinkle with salt.
5. Fix lid and bring to pressure. *Allow 18 minutes.*
6. Reduce pressure and remove lid. Check seasoning in gravy.

IRISH STEW

Times: 18 minutes for lamb chops *Serves 4*
30 minutes for older mutton chops

The perfect Irish Stew should be made in two parts: this will ensure that the final dish is fat-free. Allow 3 or 4 hours, or overnight, between the two cookings.

2 tablespoons butter or other fat
about 1½ lb (¾ kg) lamb or mutton chops. Neck would do
1 pint (½ litre) water
1 tablespoon vinegar
1 teaspoon sugar
1 bay leaf
salt and pepper to taste
3 level tablespoons flour
4 onions, peeled and quartered or 8 very small ones left whole
4 carrots, cleaned and halved
4 parsnips, cleaned and halved or quartered, according to size
about 1 lb (½ kg) potatoes, peeled and halved

First part

1. Melt the fat in the pressure pan. Trim some of the fat from the chops and fry until lightly browned. Remove pan from heat.
2. Add the water, vinegar, sugar, bay leaf and seasoning. Return to heat and fix lid. Bring to pressure and *allow 8 minutes for the lamb and 20 minutes for the mutton.*
3. Reduce pressure and remove lid. Strain broth into a bowl and put on one side for several hours or overnight. Remove chops from pan.

Second part

1. Lift the fat from the broth and put broth back into pressure pan. Mix the flour with a little cold water until smooth and stir in. Bring to the boil, stirring constantly until broth has thickened.
2. Put back the chops, then add the vegetables. Fix lid again and bring to pressure. *Allow 10 minutes for both lamb and mutton.*
3. Reduce pressure and remove lid. Taste gravy and add more salt if necessary.

LANCASHIRE HOT-POT

Times: 18 minutes for lamb chops *Serves 4*
30 minutes for mutton chops

The old traditional dish has many variations, even in Lancashire. Originally, when oysters were inexpensive, they were included. Today they are optional.

about 1½ lb (¾ kg) lamb or mutton chops, loin or neck
3 lamb kidneys, or 6 oz (150 g) ox kidney
2 large onions, peeled and chopped
1 level tablespoon flour
2 large or 4 small carrots, cleaned and sliced
1 bay leaf
4 or more potatoes, peeled and halved
1 dark stock cube or 2 teaspoons soy sauce
2 teaspoons vinegar and 1 teaspoon sugar
¼ pint (125 ml) water
salt and pepper to taste
oysters (optional)

1. Trim some of the fat from the chops. Skin kidneys, removing core and fat, and cut into slices.
2. Toss the onions in the flour.
3. Put half the chops and kidneys into pressure pan. Cover with half the onions, then half the carrots. If oysters are to be used, add about half a dozen here.
4. Repeat layers, using the rest of the four ingredients. Put in the bay leaf and arrange potatoes on top.
5. Add cube or soy sauce and the vinegar and sugar to the water. Add also 1 good teaspoon salt and a little pepper. Pour over meat and vegetables.

6. Fix lid and bring to pressure. *Allow times shown above.*
7. Reduce pressure and remove lid. Taste gravy and add more seasoning if necessary. Remove bay leaf.

PORK CHOP CASSEROLE WITH VEGETABLES

Time: 18 minutes *Serves 4*

Many people prefer a casserole without too many flavours, others love anything so long as it is interesting and different. This is a simple basic recipe and can be served as it is or with other flavours added. Use some wine if you can.

4 pork chops ¾–1 in thick
2 level tablespoons flour, or for a change use 1 heaped tablespoon packet soup, any flavour you wish, such as asparagus, mushroom or celery
1 level tablespoon butter or margarine
½ pint (250 ml) stock, or water with 1 chicken stock cube. (Half white wine may be used)
salt and pepper to taste (2 teaspoons soy sauce may replace some of the salt)
1 bay leaf, or teaspoon of any herb
celery (optional, see step 3)
large whole onions, carrots and potatoes, peeled, enough for 4

1. Trim some or all of the fat from the chops. (It could be saved and rendered down.) Dust them with the flour, using it all.
2. Melt fat in pressure pan and when hot, fry chops until lightly browned. Remove to a plate. Tip away any remaining fat.
3. Add the liquid, seasoning and herb of your choice. Put the chops back. Three or four sticks of chopped celery could be added.
4. Peel the onions and potatoes and clean the carrots. Arrange on top of the chops and sprinkle with salt.
5. Fix lid and bring to pressure. *Allow 18 minutes.*
6. Reduce pressure and remove lid. Except for a green vegetable, which could have been cooking in another saucepan, a whole meal is ready. Make sure you have added sufficient salt and pepper.

SWEET AND SOUR PORK, CHINESE STYLE

Time: 18 minutes *Serves 4*

In China pork is the most favoured of all meats and the ways of cooking it are as numerous as they are varied. The sweet-sour treatment is familiar to all Westerners who visit Chinese restaurants. This recipe brings it into your own home.

4 pork chops, about ¾ in thick
1 level tablespoon cornflour
2 good tablespoons lard or other fat
1 large onion, peeled and chopped
15½ oz (439 g) can of pineapple slices
2 level tablespoons brown sugar
1 tablespoon soy sauce
2 tablespoons vinegar
1 medium-sized green pepper, de-seeded and chopped
1 clove of garlic, crushed
a little pepper. Salt if necessary, but the soy sauce is very salty
celery in 1 in pieces (optional)

1. Trim chops and dust with the cornflour.
2. Melt the fat in the pressure pan. Fry the chops for 2 minutes on either side, then remove to a plate.
3. Tip away any surplus fat, then add the onions. Cook them for 2 minutes or until lightly browned. Remove pan from heat.
4. Measure pineapple syrup and make up to ½ pint (¼ litre) with water. Tip into pan.
5. Add the sugar, soy sauce, vinegar, green pepper, garlic and seasoning. Add also the celery if liked.
6. Stir together then return to heat. Put the chops back.
7. Fix lid and bring to pressure. *Allow 18 minutes.*
8. Heat the pineapple slices.
9. Reduce pressure and remove lid. Serve garnished with the pineapple, the centres of which could be filled with Maraschino cherries or stuffed olives. Parsley sprigs may garnish the dish.

SPICED STUFFED PORK CHOPS

Time: 20 minutes *Serves 4*

A go-further way with chops. The stuffing gives them double value and so eases the ever-mounting butcher's bill. The spices combine to give a refreshing tang to the gravy. In this recipe the chops are not fried first.

4 pork chops, about 1 in thick (see step 2)
2 teaspoons butter or margarine
2 medium-sized onions, peeled and chopped
1½ level tablespoons flour
1 level teaspoon ground ginger
½ level teaspoon curry powder
½ level teaspoon nutmeg
2 teaspoons brown sugar
¼ lb (100 g) mushrooms, washed and sliced
½ pint (¼ litre) water with 2 teaspoons soy sauce or ½ beef stock cube
salt and pepper to taste
whole potatoes and carrots

STUFFING
4 heaped tablespoons soft breadcrumbs
½ teaspoon salt and a little pepper
1 small onion, peeled and grated
½ teaspoon thyme
2 teaspoons soft butter

1. Make the stuffing by combining all the ingredients. Just chop the butter in roughly. Do not add any liquid.
2. When buying the chops ask the butcher to make a slit in each for the stuffing. Push some of it into each and secure with tiny skewers or cocktail picks.
3. Melt the butter or margarine in the pressure pan and add the chopped onions. Fry for 2 minutes.
4. Stir in the flour, spices and sugar. Remove from heat and add the mushrooms, liquid and seasoning. Mix well.
5. Put the chops into the gravy and return to heat. Arrange potatoes and carrots on top or in dividers.
6. Fix lid and bring to pressure. *Allow 20 minutes.*
7. Reduce pressure and remove lid. Check gravy for seasoning.

SUN-KISSED PORK CHOPS

Time: 18 minutes *Serves 4*

The word 'Sun-kissed' is a brand name for golden sweet oranges and so seemed appropriate for this delicious way with pork chops. Try it with veal or lamb too.

4 or more pork chops
2 good teaspoons margarine or butter
2 onions, peeled and chopped
1½ level tablespoons flour
½ pint (¼ litre) water
2 teaspoons soy sauce or 1 light stock cube
3 oranges (2 for garnish)
2 tablespoons orange curaçao
½ teaspoon sweet basil or thyme
salt and pepper to taste
1 clove of garlic, crushed (optional)
¼ lb (100 g) mushrooms washed and sliced (optional)
parsley for garnish

1. Remove rinds and some fat from the chops. Melt fat in pressure pan and fry chops until lightly browned. Remove to a plate.
2. Add onions and flour to pan and fry for 2 minutes. Remove from heat.
3. Add water and soy sauce or cube.
4. Grate the rind from one orange and squeeze out the juice. Add to pressure pan. Add also the curaçao, herb, seasoning, garlic and mushrooms if used. Mix well.
5. Put the chops back. Fix lid and bring to pressure. *Allow 18 minutes.*
6. Reduce pressure and remove lid. Slice the other two oranges and use with parsley for garnish.

A quicker way: Put fat, flour and onions into pressure pan and fry together for 1 minute. Add all the other ingredients. Fix lid and bring to pressure. *Allow the 18 minutes* and reduce pressure in the usual way.

PORK AND APPLE HOT-POT

Time: 19 minutes *Serves 6*

With the pork sandwiched between layers of onion and apple and topped with whole potatoes, the main part of a meal is all cooked together. Only the green vegetable would need another saucepan. Inexpensive spareribs may be used.

about 2½ lb (1¼ kg) pork chops or spareribs. Pork fillets, gammon or bacon could also be used. All should be cut ½–¾ in thick
1 tablespoon butter or other fat
4 medium-sized onions, peeled and chopped (see Note)
2 level tablespoons flour (see Note)

salt and pepper
4 sweet apples, peeled and sliced
a little sugar
1 dark stock cube
¼ pint (125 ml) water
whole potatoes, each 6–8 oz (150–200 g) size, peeled

1. If chops are used, cut off rind and some fat. Remove rind from gammon or bacon and cut rashers in half.
2. Melt butter or fat in pressure pan and fry the meat until browned on both sides. Lift out and put on to a plate. Remove pan from heat and tip away surplus fat.
3. Add to pan half the onions, then sprinkle with half the flour and a little salt and pepper. Cover with half the apples and sprinkle them with a little sugar, about 2 teaspoons.
4. Arrange the meat on top and sprinkle with salt and pepper.
5. Add the rest of the onions and sprinkle with the rest of the flour and a little more salt. Add the rest of the apples and sprinkle them with more sugar.
6. Stir stock cube into water and pour over everything. Arrange potatoes on top and sprinkle them with salt. Return pan to heat.
7. Fix lid and bring to pressure. *Allow 19 minutes.*
8. Reduce pressure and remove lid. Taste liquid and add more seasoning if necessary.

Note: 4 medium-sized leeks could replace the onions and celery, cut into 1 in pieces, could be added as well as the apple. *See p. 24, 'Adding whole vegetables'*. Packet soups could also replace the flour; to give added flavour use 2 rounded tablespoons.

CASSEROLED SPARERIBS

Time: 18 minutes *Serves 4–5*

Spareribs are generally the cheapest of the pork cuts and because of the way the fat is arranged, they are also tender and tasty. If you think that the gravy will be too rich in fat, cook the dish in two stages (*see steps 4 and 5 below*). Vegetables are all-in-together.

4–6 (or more) pork spareribs
2 level tablespoons flour
2 level tablespoons margarine or butter
½ pint (¼ litre) stock (or water with a chicken soup cube)
3 peeled sliced tomatoes, or ¼ pint (125 ml) canned tomatoes

2 teaspoons brown sugar
½ teaspoon basil or other herb
salt and pepper to taste (2 teaspoons soy sauce may replace some of the salt)
1 clove of garlic, crushed (optional)
small whole onions and carrots and potatoes, halved lengthwise (see Note)

1. Trim some of the fat from the spareribs and coat them with the flour.
2. Heat fat in pressure pan and fry the spareribs until lightly browned. Remove to a plate. Tip away surplus fat.
3. Add stock, tomatoes, sugar, herb, seasoning and garlic if liked. Put the spareribs back.
4. Fix lid and bring to pressure. *Allow 18 minutes if cooked in one stage and 10 if in two.*
5. Reduce pressure and remove lid. If you wish to remove all fat from the gravy, pour it into a bowl and put away until cold—the fat can then be lifted off. Put part-cooked meat on a plate and keep in refrigerator or cool place. (See the other method in the *Note* below.)
6. When fat has been removed from gravy, tip back into the pressure pan. Add the chops. Place on top small whole onions, whole carrots and potatoes, halved lengthwise, filling the pan to three-quarters capacity. Sprinkle with salt and pepper. *See p. 24.*
7. Fix lid and bring to pressure again. *Allow another 8 minutes.*
8. Reduce pressure and remove lid.

Note: If you wish to make this dish in one stage, use large whole onions, potatoes and carrots. They will not spoil if cooked for 18 minutes. Pour gravy into a tall slender jug and when fat comes to the top, it can easily be spooned off.

PORK FILLETS, BRAISED

Time: 17 minutes *Serves 4*

A bland dish for those who prefer to enjoy the delicate flavour of pork without too many additions. Only shallots, celery and parsley have been included.

1½–2 lb (¾–1 kg) pork fillets
2 level tablespoons flour
1 level tablespoon butter or margarine
4–6 shallots, or 1 Spanish onion, peeled and chopped
4–6 sticks of celery, washed and chopped
½ pint (¼ litre) water
1 chicken stock cube
3 or 4 sprigs of parsley
salt and pepper to taste

1. Trim fillets and cut each into 4 pieces. Coat with the flour.
2. Melt the fat in the pressure pan and when very hot fry the fillets until lightly browned on both sides.
3. Add shallots or onion, celery, liquid, stock cube and parsley. Season with salt and pepper.
4. Fix lid and bring to pressure. *Allow 17 minutes.*
5. Reduce pressure and remove lid. Check gravy for seasoning.

Pork fillets, curried: Add 2–4 teaspoons of curry powder with the flour. 1 or 2 peeled chopped apples may be added, in which case reduce liquid by 3 or 5 tablespoons. Raisins or sultanas may also be added.

PORK BELLY (or FLANK), SLICES

Times: 10 minutes, first stage
7 minutes, second stage
Serves 4

For price and flavour, pork belly is well worth considering. For some, the lines of fat make it too rich, but by cooking it in two stages, this can be almost wholly eliminated.

1½ lb (¾ kg) pork belly in ¾ in slices
1 level tablespoon butter or margarine
1 pint (½ litre) water
1 teaspoon salt and a little pepper
1 bay leaf
2 level tablespoons packet celery soup
2 onions, peeled and chopped
2 or 3 carrots, washed and sliced
2 teaspoons soy sauce or 1 beef stock cube

First cooking

1. Cut off the rind and the line of fat on the underside of the slices. Cut each in half.

2. Heat fat and fry slices until lightly browned. Pour off fat.
3. Add water, seasoning and bay leaf. Fix lid and bring to pressure. *Allow 10 minutes.*
4. Reduce pressure and remove lid. Lift meat on to a plate and pour broth into a bowl. Put away in refrigerator or cool place until fat has risen and become firm. Lift it off.

Second cooking

1. Put meat and broth back into pressure pan. Use 4 tablespoons of the broth to mix with the packet soup. Add this and all the other ingredients to the pressure pan.
2. Fix lid and bring to pressure. *Allow 7 minutes.*
3. Reduce pressure and remove lid. Taste and add more seasoning if necessary. Remove bay leaf.

PICKLED BELLY OF PORK

Time: 45 minutes — *Serves up to 8 depending on size*

As pressure-cooking times depend upon the thickness of food, rather than the weight, 1 lb of pork belly will take as long as 2 or 3. Because of the pickling brine, the meat takes longer to cook than fresh. Delicious served hot with sauerkraut or red cabbage or cold with a salad.

2–3 lb (1–1½ kg) pickled pork belly
water to cover
1 bay leaf
3 cloves
1 tablespoon vinegar
5 peppercorns

1. Soak the pickled pork in water to cover for a few hours, then pour the water off.
2. Rinse the pork and place on rack or trivet in pressure pan. Add 2 pints (1 litre) water and all the other ingredients.
3. Fix lid and bring to pressure. *Allow 45 minutes.*
4. Reduce pressure and remove lid. Take out the pork (the meat will have shrunk a little from the bones) and pull off the rind. If cooked sufficiently, it will slip off easily.

HAM or BACON

Time: 20 minutes to the pound *Serves up to 8*

Limit the size of your piece of ham or bacon to 3 lb; the pressure pan will then cook it to perfection. Larger pieces should be cooked in a large vessel, without pressure, or tightly sealed in a paste or several thicknesses of foil in the oven.

up to 3 lb (1½ kg) piece of ham or bacon (see above)
water to cover
2 teaspoons vinegar
3 cloves
1 bay leaf

1. Put bacon or ham into a pan and cover with water. Allow to soak for 6 hours or overnight. Drain and place on rack in pressure pan.
2. Fill pan half full with fresh water and add vinegar, cloves and bay leaf.
3. Fix lid and bring to pressure. *Allow 20 minutes for each pound.*
4. Move pan to a cool surface and let the pressure reduce gradually. Remove lid.
5. Lift out meat and remove rind. If the meat is sufficiently cooked, it will come off easily.
6. To finish, rub fatty side with brown sugar and stud with cloves. Dust with fine dry breadcrumbs. Bake in a hot oven for 15–20 minutes until the crumbs have browned. Serve with Cumberland Sauce (*p. 194*).

HAM OR BACON IN CIDER

Cook the meat as in the preceding recipe. When rind has been removed place meat in a baking dish. Preheat oven to 350 °F or gas mark 4. Pour ¾ pint (375 ml) cider over and around the meat. Bake for about 35 minutes, basting the meat twice with the cider. Remove from oven, rub fatty side with brown sugar and stud with cloves. Dust with fine dry breadcrumbs and put back into the oven until crumbs have browned. The meat looks attractive if decorated with cherries on cocktail sticks. If the ham or bacon is to be served hot make a sauce, using the cider and drippings from baking dish.

Ham or bacon with pineapple: Use pineapple juice instead of cider. The meat may be decorated with small wedges of pineapple on cocktail sticks.

BAUNTON GAMMON WITH TOMATO

Time: 15 minutes *Serves 4*

I first met this recipe when I was staying with friends in the Cotswolds. Since then I have made it many times and so gave it the name of their home, Baunton Fields.

about 1¼ lb (600 g) gammon, ½ in thick, cut into 4 pieces
2 rounded teaspoons butter or margarine
2 rounded teaspoons flour
¼ pint (125 ml) tomato juice
6 tablespoons water
1 teaspoon brown sugar, or more, according to taste
2 teaspoons Worcester sauce
a few dashes of Tabasco sauce

1. Cut rinds from gammon and soak the meat in hot water for ½ hour or longer to remove some of the salt. Rinse under the tap.
2. Melt fat in pressure pan.
3. Shake water from gammon and coat it on both sides with the flour. Use more if necessary.
4. Fry for only ½ minute on either side. Tip in the tomato juice, water, sugar, Worcester sauce and Tabasco sauce.
5. Fix lid and bring to pressure. *Allow 15 minutes.*
6. Reduce pressure and remove lid. Taste gravy and add salt if necessary: this will depend on the saltiness of the gammon.

Gammon with sweetcorn and celery: Use a small can of cream-style sweetcorn instead of the tomato juice. Add about 6 sticks of chopped celery and 6 tablespoons water. Omit the Worcester sauce.

SAUSAGES WITH A PIQUANT SAUCE

Time: 8 minutes *Serves 4*

In the method below, the sausages are fried in a frying-pan and the sauce made in the pressure pan. If however you are cooking the dish on one ring or jet, fry the sausages first in the pressure pan, then put on plate whilst you make the sauce. Potatoes and carrots may be added.

1–1½ lb (½–¾ kg) sausages or more
2 teaspoons butter or other fat
1 onion, any size, peeled and chopped
1½ level tablespoons flour
¼ pint (125 ml) stock (or water with 1 chicken cube)
½ teaspoon basil
½ lb (¼ kg) tomatoes, peeled and sliced or a can of peeled tomatoes
3 sticks of celery, trimmed and chopped (or use 1 teaspoon celery salt)
3 teaspoons brown sugar
2 teaspoons Worcester sauce
salt and pepper to taste (2 teaspoons soy sauce may replace some of the salt)

1. Prick the sausages all over. Fry in a frying-pan or in the pressure pan, using 1 teaspoon of the fat.
2. Meanwhile melt the other teaspoon of fat in the pressure pan, then add the onion and flour. Fry together for 2 minutes. Remove pan from heat.
3. Add stock, basil, tomatoes, celery (or celery salt), sugar, Worcester sauce and seasoning. Stir well and return pan to heat. Potatoes and carrots, cut small, may be added, placed in dividers or on separator.
4. Fix lid and bring to pressure. *Allow 8 minutes.*
5. Reduce pressure and remove lid. Tip in the sausages and heat through. Add more seasoning if necessary.

LIVER AND BACON

Time: 15 minutes *Serves 4*

Instead of being fried in the usual way, the liver and bacon are braised in gravy with onions and celery.

4 rashers of streaky bacon
1 lb (½ kg) calves' liver in ½ in slices
1 level tablespoon flour
2 onions, peeled and chopped
about 4 sticks of celery, trimmed and chopped
1½ gills (188 ml) of stock, or water with 1 beef stock cube
salt and pepper to taste
1 bay leaf, or ½ teaspoon thyme
1 clove of garlic, crushed (optional)

1. Remove rinds and cut the bacon into 2 in pieces. Drop into pressure pan and begin to fry.
2. Coat liver with the flour and fry with the bacon for a few minutes on either side. Add the onions and stir until they have heated through. Remove from heat.
3. Add the celery, liquid, seasoning, bay leaf or herbs and the garlic if liked. Stir, then return to heat.
4. Fix lid and bring to pressure. *Allow 15 minutes.*
5. Reduce pressure and remove lid. Check gravy for seasoning.

HEARTS, PLAIN OR STUFFED

Times: 30 minutes for sheep's hearts
40 minutes for calves' hearts
1¼ hours for ox heart

Serves 4

Provided they are cooked to perfect tenderness, hearts can be both economical and nourishing.

4 calves', 8 sheep's or 1 ox heart
1 tablespoon bacon fat or margarine
1 level tablespoon flour
½ pint (¼ litre) stock, or water with 1 beef stock cube
2 onions, peeled and chopped
salt and pepper to taste
1 tablespoon vinegar
1 level tablespoon sugar

STUFFING

2 oz (50 g) soft breadcrumbs
½ level teaspoon thyme
½ teaspoon salt and a little pepper
a little chopped parsley
2 teaspoons soft margarine

1. Remove tubes and fat from hearts. Place in a bowl of salted water and allow to soak for ½ hour or longer. This gives them a more delicate flavour. Lift out and drain.
2. If the hearts are to be stuffed, make a forcemeat by mixing all the stuffing ingredients together and mashing in the margarine roughly. Fill heart or hearts with this. Hold together with tiny skewers or thread.
3. Heat fat in the pressure pan. Roll hearts in the flour and fry in the fat, tip in any left-over flour.
4. Add liquid, onions, seasoning, vinegar and sugar. Fix lid and bring to pressure. *Allow times shown above.*

5. Reduce pressure and remove lid. Taste gravy and add more seasoning if necessary.

KIDNEYS, BRAISED

Times: 12 minutes for lamb kidneys *Serves 4*
20 minutes for ox-kidney

Lamb kidneys may be sautéd in butter in an open frying-pan and will take only 5 minutes but once they pass that time, they toughen, and so need braising.

8 rashers of bacon
1–1½ lb (½–¾ kg) lamb or ox kidneys
1 level tablespoon flour
2 onions, peeled, chopped, any size
½ pint (¼ litre) stock, or water with ½ beef stock cube (see Note)
salt and pepper to taste
2 teaspoons Worcester sauce
mushrooms, washed and sliced

1. Remove rinds and fry bacon in the pressure pan until cooked and fat has run out. Remove to a plate and keep hot.
2. Remove skin, fatty bits and cores from kidneys and cut into pieces. Roll in the flour then fry in the bacon fat in the pressure pan. Add the onion and continue frying for a minute or two. Remove from heat.
3. Add the stock, seasoning and Worcester sauce and mushrooms. Mix well, then return to heat. Fix lid and bring to pressure. *Allow 12 minutes for lamb kidneys and 20 minutes for ox kidneys.*
4. Reduce pressure and remove lid. Taste and add more seasoning if necessary. Serve with the bacon.

Note: 3 or 4 tablespoons sherry or wine, or beer, may replace some of the water.

Kidneys, devilled: Replace the water with tomatoes, either canned or fresh (using ¾ lb or 300 g), increasing Worcester sauce to 1 tablespoon and adding 1 level tablespoon brown sugar and a few dashes of Tabasco sauce, or 1 teaspoon French mustard. Excellent served with scrambled eggs.

AN ENGLISH LIVER PÂTÉ

Time: 25 minutes (2 minutes more if using a glass or china container) *Serves 6*

Traditionally, the English liver pâté was encased in pastry and called a Pâté Pie. Today we are more likely to see it uncovered and taking its place beside the pâtés from many other lands.

1 lb (½ kg) calves' or pigs' liver
½ lb (¼ kg) streaky bacon
2 medium-sized onions, or 1 Spanish onion, peeled and quartered
1 clove garlic, crushed
1 bay leaf
½ lb (¼ kg) sausage meat
1 egg, beaten
1 level teaspoon salt and a little pepper
¼ pint (125 ml) soured cream or evaporated milk
brandy (optional)

1. Have ready a loaf-tin, bowl or soufflé dish that will fit comfortably in the pressure pan.
2. Cut the skinned liver into pieces and place in a smallish saucepan. Add ¼ pint (125 ml) water.
3. Remove rinds and cut half the bacon rashers into 3 in pieces and add to liver. Add also the onions and bay leaf. Boil, covered, for 10 minutes. Drain liquid into a mixing bowl. Remove bay leaf.
4. Mince finely the liver, bacon pieces and onion and garlic. For a very smooth pâté, mince twice. Tip mixture into bowl with broth.
5. Add the sausage meat, egg and seasoning, then stir in the cream or evaporated milk. Mix well.
6. Arrange the rest of the rashers on the bottom and sides of the tin or dish; they need not completely cover the sides. Tip in the mixture and press down well. Flatten the top smoothly.
7. Put 1 pint (½ litre) of water in pressure pan and insert rack. Begin to heat.
8. Cover bowl or dish with foil and secure with a rubber band or string. Lower into pressure pan. Fix lid and bring to pressure. *Allow 25 minutes. See time above.*
9. Reduce pressure and remove lid. Lift out, remove foil and turn out on to a dish. If liked, 2 tablespoons brandy may be poured over while hot. Serve cold.

SWEETBREADS

Time: 5 minutes after blanching *Serves 4*

To prepare the sweetbreads: Soak them in cold water for 1 hour or longer to remove the blood. Lift out and rinse under the cold tap. Blanch them by putting them into a pan with a little water and 1 teaspoon vinegar and bringing to the boil for 1 minute. Strain off the water and remove skin and membrane. The sweetbreads are then ready to be used.

1 lb (½ kg) sweetbreads
¼ pint (125 ml) stock or water with ½ chicken stock cube (or half wine may be used)
1 small onion, finely chopped or grated
chopped parsley (optional)
salt and pepper to taste
Cream Sauce (p. 192); *the liquid in which the sweetbreads were cooked, made up to ½ pint (¼ litre) with milk, should be used for the sauce*

1. Prepare the sweetbreads as described above.
2. Pour the liquid into pressure pan. Cut sweetbreads into pieces and add.
3. Add onion and seasoning. Fix lid and bring to pressure. *Allow 5 minutes.*
4. Reduce pressure and remove lid. Make the Cream Sauce, adding chopped parsley if liked. Pour the sauce over the sweetbreads.

HAGGIS-IN-A-BOWL

Time: 1 hour 25 minutes *Serves 6*

Traditionally Haggis is made from the 'pluck' of the sheep (the lights, heart and liver), and cooked in the 'paunch' (the stomach bag). But Haggis cooked in a jar or bowl is also allowed. In the recipe below only one change to the Scots recipe has been made. Kidneys replace the lights or lungs.

1 sheep's heart
½ lb (¼ kg) lambs' liver
2 medium-sized onions, peeled and quartered
4 lamb kidneys
3 good tablespoons shredded suet
6 oz (150 g) coarse oatmeal (not rolled oats)

1½ teaspoons salt and plenty of black pepper
a few grains of cayenne
1 tablespoon lemon juice
¼ teaspoon ground nutmeg
½ teaspoon thyme

1. Have ready a 2–2½ pint (1–1¼ litre) bowl that will fit comfortably into the pressure pan. The Haggis will be cooked in this.
2. Cut the heart into 4 pieces and cut away the fat. Put into a large basin of salted water. Add the liver. Allow to soak for about 20 minutes to remove some of the blood.
3. Put oatmeal into grilling pan and toast under grill until a gold colour.
4. Lift out heart and liver, rinse and put into pressure pan. Remove fatty bits, skin and cores from kidneys and add to the pan. Pour in ¼ pint (125 ml) water, then fix lid and bring to pressure. *Allow 10 minutes.* Reduce pressure and remove lid.
5. Tip contents into a large mixing bowl. Mince (or pulverise in the electric blender) the meats and onion. Add to liquid in mixing bowl. Add also the suet, oatmeal, seasoning, cayenne, lemon juice, nutmeg and thyme. Stir well together.
6. Put 1 pint (½ litre) water into pressure pan and begin to heat.
7. Tip mixture into bowl and cover with foil. Tie with string or a rubber band. Lower into pressure pan and fix lid. Bring to pressure and *allow 1¼ hours.*
8. Reduce pressure and remove lid. Haggis is served!

Chicken and Game

Important note: When chickens are bought fresh it is essential to allow plenty of time for defrosting: a bird up to 4 lb in weight should thaw out in a refrigerator in up to 12 hours, rather less at room temperature, but birds over 4 lb in weight may need up to 24 hours in the refrigerator, half that at room temperature. A really small bird will thaw out overnight in the refrigerator.

TO MAKE A TOUGH FOWL TENDER FOR ROASTING

Stuff the fowl if liked, then truss and place on the rack in the pressure pan. If the bird is large it might need a little manoeuvring here and there, but don't let it press up against the vent. Add 1½ pints (¾ litre) water, 1 tablespoon lemon juice, 1 bay leaf, 1 onion, peeled and halved and 2 teaspoons salt. Fix the lid and bring to pressure. *Allow 30 minutes.* (In the meantime heat the oven, putting in a baking dish with fat in 10 minutes before the end of pressure-cooking time.) Reduce pressure and remove lid. Lift out the bird, shake off the broth and roast in the usual way until tender, basting twice. Potatoes may, of course, be roasted at the same time. Some of the broth may be used for gravy, the rest as the stock for soups.

CHICKEN, BRAISE-ROASTED

Times: 22 minutes for a 3 lb (1½ kg) chicken *Serves 4–6*
25 minutes for a 3½–4 lb (1¾–2 kg) chicken

To be true to the name 'Roast Chicken', we should 'dry' cook it in the oven or on a spit. In a pressure pan we can first brown it, then cook it to perfect tenderness and finish with a honey glaze in the oven.

a 3–4 lb (1½–2 kg) roasting chicken
forcemeat, or rice, mushrooms and prune stuffing (p. 196)
3 tablespoons oil or other fat
water
salt and pepper
streaky bacon rashers for garnish
2 teaspoons clear honey
bread sauce
½ teaspoon tarragon or other herb

1. Wash and trim the giblets, removing the gall bladder. Leave them in a cup of water.
2. Make the stuffing and fill the inside of the chicken. Close the cavity with tiny skewers or needle and thread. Truss the bird as it was when bought.
3. Heat the oil or other fat in the pressure pan and brown the bird well all over. Lift it out and put on a plate. Tip the fat into the oven baking dish.

4. Put the giblets and water into the pressure pan. Add another ¾ pint (375 ml) water. Add the herb, 1 teaspoon salt and a little pepper. Insert rack and put the bird on it.
5. Fix lid and bring to pressure. *Allow times shown above.*
6. Meanwhile heat the oven to 425 °F or gas mark 5. Remove rinds from 3 or 4 rashers of bacon, cut each rasher in two and roll up. Put on an enamel plate or other shallow oven dish.
7. Reduce pressure and remove lid. Put chicken into oven baking dish and baste at once with the fat. Smear breasts with honey and bake in a moderate oven for about 15 minutes or until honey has added a roasted look to the bird. Cook the bacon rolls at the same time.
8. Strain the broth and use some of it to make the gravy in the usual way.
9. Put the bird on a heated serving dish and surround with the bacon rolls. Serve with bread sauce.

Note: Scalloped Potatoes (*p. 155*) could be cooked earlier in the day in the pressure pan, then placed in the oven to be reheated and browned with the chicken.

CHICKEN WITH TARRAGON AND LEMON

Times: 22 minutes for a 3 lb (1½ kg) chicken *Serves 4–6*
25 minutes for a 3½–4 lb (1¾–2 kg) chicken

An elegant recipe for a special occasion. The bird will emerge browned and unusually flavoured.

1 3–4 lb (1½–2 kg) roasting chicken
1 pint (½ litre) water
1 large lemon
6 sprigs of fresh tarragon, or 1 teaspoon dried
3 level tablespoons butter or margarine, or oil
2 tablespoons brandy
1 medium-sized onion, peeled and chopped
2 level tablespoons flour
1 teaspoon sugar
1 clove of garlic, crushed (optional)
salt and pepper to taste
4 oz (100 g) mushrooms, washed and sliced
4 tablespoons soured or fresh cream

1. Wash and trim giblets, removing gall bladder, and place them

in a saucepan with 1 pint (½ litre) water. Cover and simmer for about 10 minutes.
2. Cut the lemon in half and squeeze out the juice. Put half the skin into the bird with half the tarragon and 1 tablespoon of the butter. Truss the bird.
3. Heat the rest of the fat in the pressure pan and brown the bird in it. Lift out and put on to a plate. Tip away fat.
4. Pour the brandy into the pressure pan. Flame the brandy and when the flame has died down, add the onion and flour. Cook together for 2 minutes, then remove from heat and stir in the broth from the giblets.
5. Add the lemon juice, sugar, garlic, seasoning and the remainder of the tarragon. Stir well and then return to heat.
6. Insert rack and put the bird on it. Fix lid and bring to pressure. *Allow times shown above.*
7. Meanwhile fry the mushrooms in a little butter.
8. Reduce pressure and remove lid. Strain broth and use about ½ pint (¼ litre) for the gravy, skimming off fat if necessary. Add the cream and mushrooms and serve this sauce separately. Use the rest of the broth as a basis for soup, removing the fat when cold.

CHICKEN or BOILING FOWL, STEAMED

Times: 22 minutes for a 3 lb (1½ kg) chicken *Serves 4–8*
25 minutes for a 3½–4 lb (1¾–2 kg) chicken
40–45 minutes for a 4–5 lb (2–2½ kg) boiling fowl

A steamed bird is useful for many occasions. Served with a sauce it makes a change from roasting and for a cold picnic meal or for chicken in aspic it is tender and impregnated with subtle flavours.

1 trussed chicken or fowl of a size that will fit comfortably in your pressure pan
1½ pints (¾ litre) water
1 large or 2 smaller onions, peeled and halved
1 bay leaf
3 or 4 sticks of celery, cleaned and chopped, or 1 teaspoon celery salt
½ teaspoon thyme or tarragon
1 good teaspoon salt and a little pepper

1. Wash and trim giblets, removing gall bladder. Rinse inside of bird, then place on rack in pressure pan.
2. Add the water, onions, bay leaf, celery or celery salt, herb and seasoning. Add the giblets.
3. Fix lid and bring to pressure. *Allow times shown above.*
4. Reduce pressure and remove lid.
5. Carefully lift out the bird and keep hot. The broth may be strained and used for soup; when cold, lift off the fat.
6. The vegetables may be added to a Cream Sauce (*p. 192*) and served with the bird. Use part broth and part milk. Chopped parsley may be added.

CHICKEN or BOILING FOWL CASSEROLE

Times: 18–20 minutes for chicken (average) *Serves 4*
30 minutes for boiling fowl of uncertain age

This is a quick and simple dish. To save preparation time, the preliminary frying of the chicken has been eliminated and colour is given to the dish by the gravy.

2–2½ lb (1–1¼ kg) disjointed chicken or boiling fowl
2 level tablespoons flour with ½ teaspoon salt
1 rounded teaspoon butter, margarine, or other fat
2–3 onions, any size, peeled and chopped
½ teaspoon thyme or bouquet garni
2 teaspoons soy sauce or 1 teaspoon vegetable concentrate
salt and pepper to taste
1 clove of garlic, crushed (optional)
¾ pint (375 ml) stock, or water with 1 chicken stock cube (or half wine may be used)

1. Trim the chicken, removing as much fat as possible. Put the flour and salt into a paper bag and add the chicken, two pieces at a time. Shake until evenly coated with the flour.
2. Melt the fat in the pan and add the onions. Fry for 2 minutes, then put in the chicken.
3. Add extra vegetables, if liked, herb, soy sauce or vegetable concentrate and seasoning, including garlic if used. If extra vegetables

have been added, the liquid could be reduced to ½ pint. Pour it in. Whole large potatoes could be placed on top of the chicken and cooked at the same time. Sprinkle them with salt.
4. Fix lid and bring to pressure. *Allow times shown above.*
5. Reduce pressure and remove lid. Check gravy for seasoning.

Chicken with asparagus: Use the liquid from freshly-cooked or canned asparagus instead of some of the stock or water, and the spears for a garnish. A fine party dish.

COQ AU VIN

Times: 18–20 minutes *Serves 4*
12 minutes if chicken very young

Another traditional French dish, flavoured with red Burgundy or Beaujolais. It is typical of the provincial cooking of Burgundy and has become famous in good restaurants in most parts of the world.

2–2½ lb (1–1¼ kg) disjointed chicken
2 rashers of streaky bacon
1 level tablespoon butter, oil or other fat
1 medium-sized onion, peeled and chopped, or 1 tablespoon dried onions with 3 tablespoons water
2 level tablespoons flour
½ pint (¼ litre) Burgundy or Beaujolais. (Part stock or water could be used)
½ teaspoon mixed herbs
salt and pepper to taste
4 oz (100 g) button mushrooms, washed, or use canned mushrooms (see Note)
1 clove of garlic, crushed (optional)

1. Trim the chicken, removing as much of the fat as possible.
2. Remove rind and cut the bacon into 1 in pieces. Drop into pressure pan and begin to fry. Add the fat. Fry for 3 minutes.
3. Add the chicken, two pieces at a time and fry until lightly browned. Remove to a plate.
4. Add the onion if fresh is being used (leave the dried ones until later) and fry for about 2 minutes, then sprinkle in the flour and mix. Remove from heat.
5. Add the liquid, including dried onions and water if used, the herbs and seasoning. Stir well.

6. Return to heat and add the chicken and mushrooms, with garlic if liked. If a darker gravy is preferred, add 2 teaspoons soy sauce or ½ stock cube.
7. Fix lid and bring to pressure. *Allow 18–20 minutes or 12 if a very young bird.*
8. Reduce pressure and remove lid. Check gravy for seasoning.

Note: If you use canned mushrooms the liquid will increase the quantity of gravy, so if you prefer a richer gravy, omit the juice and save it for soup.

POULET AUX CHAMPIGNONS

Time: 18–20 minutes (average age bird) *Serves 4*

Another traditional French dish, of which the two main features are mushrooms and soured cream. Chefs and housewives have their own variations, adding to or changing some of the ingredients. Here the dish is both quickly prepared and quickly cooked.

2–2½ lb (1–1¼ kg) disjointed chicken
1 level tablespoon butter or margarine, or oil
1 heaped tablespoon packet celery soup
a 10½ oz (268 g) can of cream of mushroom soup
4 tablespoons sherry (or extra water)
salt and pepper to taste (2 teaspoons soy sauce could replace some of the salt)
4 oz (100 g) white button mushrooms, washed
1 clove of garlic, crushed (optional)
4 tablespoons soured cream

1. Trim chicken, cutting away as much of the fat as possible.
2. Heat fat in pressure pan and fry chicken, two pieces at a time, until lightly browned. Remove to a plate.
3. To the pressure pan add the celery soup, mushroom soup, sherry, seasoning, mushrooms and, if liked, the garlic. Mix well.
4. Add the chicken.
5. Fix lid and bring to pressure. *Allow 18–20 minutes.*
6. Reduce pressure and remove lid. Add the soured cream. Check gravy for seasoning.

CURRIED CHICKEN, BENGAL STYLE

Time: 18–20 minutes *Serves 4*

If you live in the vicinity of an Indian food shop, you will smell the irresistible aroma of the various spices on sale. In this recipe they are used separately to combine for an authentic Indian curry. Served with boiled rice (*p. 198*).

4 chicken legs or about 2–2½ lb (1–1¼ kg) disjointed chicken
1 level tablespoon butter or margarine, or oil
1 level tablespoon flour
½ pint (¼ litre) stock or water with 1 chicken stock cube
1 heaped tablespoon desiccated coconut
2 tablespoons lemon juice
1 teaspoon brown sugar
2 medium-sized onions, peeled and chopped
1 clove of garlic, crushed (optional)
salt and pepper to taste
chopped celery (optional)

CURRY MIXTURE
2 level teaspoons ground coriander
1 level teaspoon ground turmeric
½ level teaspoon ground cummin seed
½ level teaspoon ground chillis

1. Combine ingredients for curry powder.
2. Trim chicken, cutting away as much fat as possible.
3. Melt the fat in the pressure pan and add curry powder and flour. Fry together for 2 minutes.
4. Put in the chicken pieces then add the stock or water, the coconut, lemon juice, sugar, onions, garlic, if used, and seasoning. A few sticks of celery, chopped, may be added.
5. Mix well, then fix lid and bring to pressure. *Allow 18–20 minutes.*
6. Reduce pressure and remove lid. Check gravy for seasoning.

CHICKEN MARENGO

Time: 18–20 minutes *Serves 4*

One might wonder why a chicken dish should be called after a battle-field! But there is a reason. While Napoleon was attacking the Austrians, his chef was back at headquarters trying to find a new way to cook the chickens he had pinched from the nearest poultry farm. In the garden there was a glut of tomatoes, ripe and asking to be used, so he did the obvious thing and came up with this recipe.

about 2–2½ lb (1–1¼ kg) chicken legs, or disjointed chicken
2 level tablespoons butter or other fat or oil
2 medium-sized onions, peeled and chopped. Leeks may be used instead, or as well
2 level tablespoons flour
¾ lb (300 g) tomatoes peeled, fresh or canned
¼ pint (125 ml) white wine, or the same of water with 2 teaspoons lemon juice and 2 teaspoons sugar
½ teaspoon basil or other herb
¼ lb (100 g) mushrooms, washed and halved
salt and pepper to taste (2 teaspoons soy sauce may replace some of the salt)
1 clove of garlic, crushed (optional)

1. Trim chicken, cutting off as much fat as possible.
2. Melt fat in pressure pan and fry the chicken, two or three pieces at a time until lightly browned. Put on to a plate. Tip away all but a coating of the fat.
3. Add onions and stir for 2 minutes, then add the flour and cook for another minute. Remove from heat.
4. Add tomatoes, liquid, herb, mushrooms, seasoning and garlic, if liked. Stir well together then return to heat.
5. Put the chicken back. Fix lid and bring to pressure. *Allow 18–20 minutes.*
6. Reduce pressure and remove lid. Check gravy for seasoning.

CHICKEN LIVERS

Time: 6 minutes *Serves 4*

Chicken livers are inexpensive and delicately flavoured. They are good served with scrambled eggs.

2 teaspoons butter, oil or margarine
1 lb (½ kg) chicken livers
1 level tablespoon flour or 1 rounded tablespoon packet soup (mushroom, celery or asparagus)
1 medium-sized onion, peeled and chopped
½ pint (¼ litre) water or use half wine

1 tablespoon lemon juice and 1 rounded teaspoon sugar (unless wine is used)
1 teaspoon soy sauce or ½ beef stock cube
salt and pepper to taste
1 clove of garlic, crushed (optional)
parsley, chopped, for garnish

1. Melt butter or oil in pressure pan.
2. Trim livers and cut into pieces. Tip into pressure pan with the flour or packet soup. Fry until lightly browned.
3. Add onions and fry for another minute, then add liquid with lemon juice and sugar unless wine has been used. Add soy sauce or stock cube, garlic, if liked, and seasoning.
4. Fix lid and bring to pressure. *Allow 6 minutes.*
5. Reduce pressure and remove lid. Taste and add more seasoning if necessary. Sprinkle with chopped parsley.

Chicken livers with sherry: Replace 3 tablespoons of the water with sherry. Add also 1 teaspoon made mustard or French mustard. Omit lemon juice and sugar.

Chicken livers with mushrooms and tomatoes: Add 4 oz (100 g) or more button mushrooms, replacing the water with ½ pint (¼ kg) of canned Italian peeled tomatoes, or a few peeled sliced fresh ones. Add 2 teaspoons sugar and 1 teaspoon Worcester sauce, omitting lemon juice.

TURKEY AND HAM UPSIDE-DOWN MEAT LOAF

Time: 20 minutes *Serves 5–6*

A quick way to use up some of that left-over Christmas turkey and ham. It makes an attractive-looking loaf which, when turned out, reveals your decorative handiwork.

about 1½ lb (¾ kg) cooked turkey and ham, in any proportion
1 medium-sized onion, peeled
2 oz (50 g) fresh breadcrumbs
1 egg, beaten
salt and pepper to taste
2 teaspoons butter
2 teaspoons brown sugar
1 small can of pineapple rings in syrup
a few cocktail cherries

1. Have ready a cake tin about 2½–3 in deep that will fit comfortably in your pressure pan; a round one 6–6½ in across, or a smaller square one, or a loaf tin.
2. Mince together the turkey, ham and onion. Add the breadcrumbs, egg and a little salt and pepper. The amount will depend upon the quantity and saltiness of the ham.
3. Melt the butter and pour into tin. Sprinkle on the sugar.
4. Open the can of pineapple and add 4 tablespoons of the syrup to the turkey and ham mixture. Stir all together.
5. Make a pattern of the pineapple slices and cocktail cherries on the bottom of the tin. One whole pineapple ring could go in the middle and be surrounded by halves. Press in the mixture. Cover with foil and secure with a rubber band or string.
6. Pour ½ pint (¼ litre) water into pressure pan and insert rack or trivet. Lower the tin on to it. Fix lid and bring to pressure. *Allow 20 minutes.*
7. Reduce pressure and remove lid. Lift out tin, remove foil and turn loaf out. Serve hot or cold.

GUINEA FOWL, BRAISED

Time: 15–18 minutes *Serves 4*

A guinea fowl is similar in size to a chicken but has longer legs and slate-coloured plumage with small white spots. The flesh is similar in colour to the pheasant and is tender, with a somewhat 'gamey' flavour.

1 guinea fowl, trussed
2 rashers streaky bacon
1 level tablespoon butter or margarine
1 medium-sized onion, peeled and chopped
1 level tablespoon flour
½ pint (¼ litre) stock or water with 1 chicken stock cube
½ teaspoon mixed herbs
1 carrot, sliced
salt and pepper to taste

1. Remove rind and cut bacon into 2 in pieces. Drop into pressure pan. Begin to fry, then add butter or margarine and continue frying until fat runs from bacon.
2. Brown the guinea fowl in the fat, then remove to a plate.

3. Add onion and flour and cook together for 2 or 3 minutes. Move pan from heat.
4. Add stock, herbs, carrot and seasoning. Mix well.
5. Insert rack and put the bird on it. Return to heat and fix lid.
6. Bring to pressure. *Allow 15–18 minutes.*
7. Reduce pressure and remove lid. Place bird on a heated serving dish. Strain gravy and serve separately.

BRAISED DUCKLING WITH ORANGES

Time: 16 minutes for duckling *Serves 4–6*

Because of the excessive fat in ducks, it would be wise to make this dish in two stages, perhaps one the day before. All the fat could thus be easily removed.

1 duckling, disjointed
2 level tablespoons butter or margarine (or oil)
2 level tablespoons flour
2 medium-sized onions, peeled and sliced
½ pint (¼ litre) water
3 large oranges
3 tablespoons curaçao
½ teaspoon rosemary
salt and pepper to taste
2 teaspoons soy sauce or ½ beef stock cube
¼ lb (100 g) mushrooms, washed and sliced (optional)
3 sticks of celery, chopped (optional)

1. Disjoint duckling, then remove skin and trim.
2. Melt the fat in the pressure pan and when very hot brown the duckling. Remove to a plate. Tip away surplus fat.
3. Add the flour and onions and fry together for 2 minutes. Remove from heat.
4. Add the water, the juice and grated rind of one of the oranges, the curaçao, rosemary and seasoning, including soy sauce or cube. Stir together and return to heat.
5. Put the duckling pieces back. Fix lid and bring to pressure. *Allow only 10 minutes.*
6. Reduce pressure and remove lid. Lift out duckling and pour the gravy into a bowl. Put this away until cold and the fat has solidified and can be removed.
7. Pour gravy back into pressure pan. If you need more gravy, add a

little more water. Chopped celery and washed sliced mushrooms could be added now. Put the duckling pieces back. Fix lid again and bring to pressure. *Allow the other 6 minutes.*

8. Reduce pressure and remove lid. Check gravy for seasoning. Peel and slice the other two oranges. Put duckling pieces on a heated dish and surround with the oranges. Serve the gravy separately.

Braised duckling with cherries: Follow main recipe using one 15½ oz (425 g) can of sweetened black or red cherries. Replace orange juice with 2 tablespoons lemon juice and 3 tablespoons cherry syrup. Replace the curaçao with dry sherry. Stone the cherries, heat through in a little syrup and use as a garnish instead of the two oranges.

Duckling marinated: Follow main recipe but first marinate the duckling pieces in a mixture of ½ pint (¼ litre) red wine, ¼ pint (125 ml) water, 1 onion peeled and halved, 1 crushed clove of garlic (optional), 1 bay leaf and a little salt and pepper. Leave for 4 or more hours, or overnight, turning twice. Use this strained marinade liquid instead of the water. Omit the curaçao.

HARE IN PORT WINE WITH FORCEMEAT BALLS

Time: 30 minutes *Serves 6*

In this recipe the legs and forelegs (wings) only have been used. The back is ideal for stuffing and roasting. If you are disjointing the hare yourself, be careful to save the blood that has collected in the ribs under a membrane. It is used to thicken the gravy.

the legs and wings of 1 hare
4 oz (100 g) streaky bacon
3 medium-sized onions, peeled and chopped
1 rounded teaspoon flour (see Note)
½ teaspoon thyme
salt and pepper to taste (2 teaspoons soy sauce may replace some of the salt)
blood of the hare (see Note)
redcurrant jelly, for serving

MARINADE

½ pint (¼ litre) port wine
¼ pint (125 ml) water
2 bay leaves
1 tablespoon oil
4 crushed juniper berries

FORCEMEAT BALLS

Mix together:

4 oz (2 cups or 100 g) fresh breadcrumbs

1 teaspoon thyme

¼ teaspoon salt and a little pepper

1 tablespoon chopped parsley

1 small onion, peeled and grated

1 beaten egg

1. Disjoint hare. Rinse, wipe dry, then put into marinade mixture. Leave for several hours or overnight, turning twice.
2. Remove rinds from bacon and cut into 2 in pieces. Drop into pressure pan and fry until fat runs out.
3. Lift out hare pieces and fry in the bacon fat until lightly browned. Remove to a plate.
4. Add onions and fry for 3 minutes, then stir in the flour. Remove from heat.
5. Add marinade mixture and mix well. Add the hare, then the thyme and seasoning.
6. Fix lid and bring to pressure. *Allow 30 minutes.*
7. Meanwhile mix the forcemeat ingredients together and form into little balls. Fry them in butter or margarine until lightly browned all over.
8. Reduce pressure and remove lid. Lift out hare and place on heated serving dish.
9. Move pressure pan from heat and slowly add the blood, stirring to thicken the gravy.
10. Taste gravy and add more seasoning if necessary. Pour a little over the hare and serve the rest in a sauceboat. Garnish with the forcemeat balls and, if liked, some watercress or parsley. Serve with redcurrant jelly.

Note: If the blood is to be omitted, increase flour to 2 level tablespoons.

RABBIT STEW

Time: 25 minutes *Serves 4–5*

A simple casserole-style rabbit dish flavoured with bacon, onions, celery and herbs.

about 2–2½ lb (1–1¼ kg) disjointed rabbit (the best parts)
2 rashers streaky bacon (or more if you wish)
1 level tablespoon butter, margarine or oil
2 medium-sized onions, peeled and chopped
2 level tablespoons flour
½ pint (¼ litre) stock, or water with a chicken stock cube
½ teaspoon mixed herbs or bouquet garni
4 sticks of celery, trimmed and cut into 1 in pieces
salt and pepper to taste

1. Put the rabbit into a basin of salted water and soak for about ½ hour or longer.
2. Remove rinds and cut bacon into 2 in pieces. Drop into pressure pan. Add the fat and fry together for 2 minutes.
3. Lift out the rabbit joints and dry with kitchen paper. Fry in the pan with the bacon, two pieces at a time, until lightly browned. Put them on to a plate.
4. Add onions to pan and fry for 1 minute, then sprinkle in the flour and mix well.
5. Add the liquid, herbs, celery and seasoning. Stir together.
6. Put the rabbit back. Fix lid and bring to pressure. *Allow 25 minutes.*
7. Reduce pressure and remove lid. Check gravy for seasoning.

Curried rabbit: Add 3–4 teaspoons curry powder with the flour. Include 2 chopped apples and 4 tablespoons sultanas. Serve with boiled rice (*p. 198*) and other accompaniments (*p. 94*).

CREAMED RABBIT

Time: 25 minutes *Serves 4–5*

This recipe is often used to make rabbit pie. If you would like to do this, reduce time to 18 minutes. The rabbit will continue cooking in the oven. A Rabbit Pie recipe follows this one.

1 medium-sized rabbit, disjointed
3 rashers streaky bacon
1½ level tablespoons flour
2 onions (any size), peeled and sliced
¾ cup (187 ml) water
4–6 sticks of celery, trimmed and cut into 1 in pieces
1 bay leaf
salt and pepper to taste

1 or 2 cloves of garlic, crushed (optional)
¼ pint (125 ml) water
¼ pint (125 ml) top of milk or cream
1 tablespoon chopped parsely

1. Soak rabbit in salted water for ½ hour or longer.
2. Remove rind and cut bacon into 2 in pieces and drop into pressure pan. Fry until fat begins to run out.
3. Add flour and onions and cook for 2 minutes. Remove from heat.
4. Add the water, celery, bay leaf and seasoning. Add also the garlic if liked. Stir well then return to heat.
5. Lift rabbit from water and drain well. Add to pressure pan.
6. Fix lid and bring to pressure. *Allow 25 minutes.*
7. Reduce pressure and remove lid. Add top of milk or cream. More than the ¼ pint may be added if more gravy is wanted. Add the parsley. Taste and add more seasoning if necessary.

Creamed rabbit pie: Make the creamed rabbit, but allow 18 minutes instead of 25. Tip into pie dish, cover with shortcrust or puff pastry and bake for 40 minutes in a moderate oven.

RABBIT FRICASSEE, SPANISH STYLE

Time: 25 minutes *Serves 4–5*

It is not uncommon to find in Spanish cooking the use of honey or grated chocolate in meat dishes. Here honey is used to enhance the flavour of the tomatoes or pimentos, but if you feel adventurous, try the chocolate (1 oz or 25 g).

about 2–2½ lb (1–1¼ kg) disjointed rabbit (choose the best parts)
2–4 rashers streaky bacon
1 level tablespoon butter or margarine or oil
2 medium-sized onions, or 1 large Spanish, peeled and chopped
2 level tablespoons flour
¼ pint (125 ml) water
¼ pint (125 ml) either white wine, cider or light ale or ¼ pint (125 ml) water with 1 tablespoon lemon juice
1 good tablespoon clear honey
½ lb (¼ kg) tomatoes, peeled, or 3 canned pimentos with 2 tablespoons of the liquor
½ teaspoon basil or other herb
1 clove of garlic, crushed (optional)
salt and pepper to taste

1. Soak the rabbit in a basin of salted water for about ½ hour.
2. Remove rinds and cut bacon into 3 in pieces. Drop into the pressure pan with the fat and begin to fry.
3. Add the onions and fry with the bacon until lightly browned. Sprinkle in the flour and stir. Remove from heat.
4. Add the liquid, honey, tomatoes or pimentos, herbs, seasoning and garlic if used. Stir everything together. Return to heat.
5. Drain the rabbit well and put into the gravy. Fix lid and bring to pressure. *Allow 25 minutes.*
6. Reduce pressure and remove lid. Check gravy for seasoning.

BRAISED PIGEONS

Times: 25 minutes, average age *Serves 4*
40 minutes for older birds

If you could discover the secret lives of the pigeons, you would be able to judge the cooking times exactly. Prepared birds bought at a reputable shop are usually tenderised in 25 minutes. Younger than average would only need about 15 minutes.

4 prepared pigeons
4 rashers streaky bacon
2 medium-sized onions, peeled and chopped
1½ level tablespoons flour
mushrooms, washed and halved (optional)
¼ pint (125 ml) red wine
½ pint (250 ml) water
2 teaspoons soy sauce or 1 beef stock cube
½ teaspoon thyme
salt and pepper to taste

1. Cut pigeons down the centre with a sharp knife, wash, then remove the sharp little breast bones. Cut off the meatless leg joints. Put these bones into a saucepan with the water and simmer for 10 minutes.
2. Remove rinds and cut bacon into 2 in pieces. Drop into pressure pan and begin to fry gently. Add onions and continue to fry for 2 minutes.
3. Sprinkle in the flour and mix with bacon, onions and mushrooms, if used. Pour in the strained stock from the little bones. Add wine, soy sauce, or cube, thyme and seasoning.

4. Mix well then put in the pigeons. Fix lid and bring to pressure. *Allow time shown above.*
5. Reduce pressure and remove lid. Check gravy for seasoning.

VENISON, BRAISE-ROASTED

Times: 20 minutes per lb *Serves up to 8*
5 minutes for the marinade

If, after several days hanging, the venison is put into a marinade and impregnated for 36–48 hours, the flavour is improved and the meat partly tenderised.

2–3 lb (1–1½ kg) of venison

MARINADE
1 medium-sized onion, peeled and sliced
2 sticks of celery, trimmed and cut into 1 in pieces
½ pint (¼ litre) wine
½ pint (¼ litre) water
1 bay leaf and ½ teaspoon thyme
4 cloves
juice of 1 large lemon

1. Put all the marinade ingredients into the pressure pan. Fix lid and bring to pressure. *Allow 5 minutes.*
2. Reduce pressure and remove lid. Tip marinade into a deep dish, large enough to hold the venison. Allow to cool completely.
3. Put in the venison and allow to marinate for 36–48 hours, turning now and again.
4. Heat 3 tablespoons oil or other fat in pressure pan. Lift out venison and dry with kitchen paper. Brown in the fat on all sides. Lift out meat and discard fat.
5. Put rack into pressure pan and pour in ½ pint (¼ litre) of the marinade and an extra ¼ pint (125 ml) water. Add the vegetables and 1 teaspoon salt.
6. Fix lid and bring to pressure. *Allow time given.*
7. Reduce pressure and remove lid. Lift out the meat and keep it warm. Use as much broth as is needed for gravy and thicken with flour mixed with cold water until smooth. Serve venison with redcurrant jelly.

4. Vegetables and Vegetable Dishes

When the first modern pressure pans were introduced and took the place of the old heavy pressure cookers (known and used for 200 years), dividers for the multiple cooking of vegetables were not supplied, and the only extra was the rack.

Dividers then began to appear and users were advised to cook three vegetables at the same time. Unfortunately this brought problems. Firstly it was found that the amount of vegetable each of the three dividers would hold was too small for even a family of four, and secondly that only root vegetables would take similar times. This meant that if a green vegetable was to be put into the third divider, all the pressure-cooking process had to be repeated half-way through the cooking of the root vegetables. (And some manufacturers now only supply two dividers.) It was soon realised that the time saved in the pressure-cooking of green vegetables was hardly worth the bother and that it was better to cook them separately in another saucepan. Only in tiny flats or bedsits where there is only one burner is it worthwhile opening up the pan and going through the process of inserting a green vegetable. Remember though, that unlike the root vegetables which are unharmed if overcooked by a few minutes, green vegetables would be ruined even if overcooked by ten seconds, so it really is best to cook them in an ordinary saucepan.

The following timings are given for those vegetables I consider worth pressure-cooking:

GENERAL INSTRUCTIONS FOR COOKING VEGETABLES

Use ¼ pint (125 ml) water for vegetables needing from 1 to 10 minutes cooking. For vegetables needing longer times, allow ½ pint (¼ litre). Add salt before cooking and reduce pressure at once with cold water. Although root vegetables will come to no harm if given a few minutes over, this doesn't mean that they can be treated with reckless abandon!

Artichokes, globe: 7–10 minutes according to size.

Artichokes, Jerusalem: 4 minutes if halved, 6–8 if whole.

Beans, broad (shelled): 5 minutes.

Beans, broad (whole and very young): 5 minutes.

Beans, dried: (*See p. 197.*)

Beetroot: 1–1½ in diameter, 12 minutes, 2 in diameter, 20 minutes, 2½ in diameter, 25–30 minutes. Use ½–¾ pint (250–375 ml) water, according to time needed.

Brussels sprouts: 4–5 minutes, time exactly.

Carrots (young, small and whole): 6 minutes. Older carrots, halved lengthwise, or sliced, 8 minutes. In stews they will not spoil, even if pressure-cooked for 25 minutes.

Cauliflower: If whole, 5 minutes.

Celeriac: Sliced, 5 minutes.

Celery: 4–5 minutes, cut into 1–3 in pieces.

Chicory: 6 minutes.

Corn-on-the-cob: Only cook if young and fresh. Remove leaves and silk. Cook whole for 5 minutes.

Kohl-rabi: Peel and slice. Pressure-cook for 5 minutes. The leaves and stems may be chopped and cooked separately. Allow 5 minutes.

Onions: Sliced thinly, 6 minutes. Whole 10–15 minutes according to size.

Parsnips: As carrots.

Potatoes: ½–¾ in slices, 4 minutes; whole about 1¼–1½ in in diameter and large halved lengthwise, 8 minutes; 2 in in diameter, 10 minutes; 2½ in in diameter, 15 minutes; these, and up to 3 in in diameter, may be cooked for up to 20 minutes in a casserole-style dish.

Pumpkin: Cut in 1½ in pieces, 5 minutes.

Salsify: Cut into 4 in pieces, 8 minutes. (Put a little lemon juice in the water.)

Swedes: As turnips.

Sweet potatoes or kumaras: As ordinary potatoes.

Sweetcorn: (*See Corn-on-the-cob*)

Turnips: 5 minutes if small, 8–10 minutes if larger.

A FEW VEGETABLE DISHES

Beets with sweet-sour sauce: Use small sweet beetroot. Pressure-cook as directed and remove skins. Make Sweet-sour Sauce (*p. 195*) and pour over.

Candied carrots: Pressure-cook the carrots as directed. Drain. For 1 lb (½ kg) carrots use the following syrup: Melt 1 tablespoon margarine or butter in a pan, add 2 tablespoons golden syrup. When melted together, add the carrots and cook for about 5 minutes, turning frequently until well coated. Sprinkle with chopped mint.

Celery and onion with soured cream: Pressure-cook celery as directed, but with 1 grated or finely chopped onion. Drain and tip into serving dish. Pour over about ¼ pint (125 ml) soured cream. Sprinkle with chopped parsley.

Chicory sweet-sour with olives: Pressure-cook young chicory as directed. Drain. Tip into serving dish and sprinkle with 1 level dessertspoon sugar to 1 lb (½ kg) chicory. Pour over about ¼ pint (125 ml) soured cream and sprinkle with sliced stuffed olives.

Sweet potatoes, glazed: Pressure-cook the sweet potatoes, giving them the same pressure-cooking time as ordinary potatoes. Melt together 2 tablespoons butter and 2 tablespoons brown sugar. Drain potatoes and add. Cook for about 5 minutes, turning until lightly browned and glazed.

Stuffed marrow: Peel and cut one end off. Scoop out seeds. Fill with a stuffing made with ½ lb (¼ kg) chopped or minced meat or fish, 2–3 oz (50–75 g) breadcrumbs, 1 grated onion, ½ teaspoon thyme, salt and pepper and 2 teaspoons butter. Skewer back the end of the marrow. Put on rack in pressure pan, add ½ pint water and 1 teaspoon salt, bring to pressure and *allow 12 minutes.*

Salsify fritters: Pressure-cook the salsify as directed. Make a fritter batter. Cut the cooked salsify into ½ in pieces and stir into batter. The flavour is said to resemble oysters, so if you wish to create the illusion add plenty of salt or a little anchovy sauce to the batter. Fry in very hot fat until crisp and browned.

SCALLOPED POTATOES

Time: 35 minutes *Serves 4*

This recipe is a treasure for the cook-hostess faced with those last minute dishing-up problems. The potatoes are thinly sliced, layered with flour, butter, milk and seasoning, and cooked in a dish that can be brought to the table.

about 1½ lb (¾ kg) potatoes
3 heaped teaspoons flour
3 rounded teaspoons butter
salt and pepper
8 tablespoons milk
topping (see step 7)

1. Have ready a dish or bowl that will fit comfortably in the pressure pan and is good enough to be brought to the table.

2. Peel the potatoes and cut into ⅛ in slices. Put one-third in the dish. Sprinkle with 1 teaspoon of the flour and dot with 1 teaspoon of the butter in little pieces. Sprinkle with salt and pepper and add 2 tablespoons of the milk.
3. Repeat this layer twice more, adding the last 4 tablespoons of the milk to the top layer.
4. Pour 1 pint (½ litre) water into pressure pan and insert rack. Begin to heat.
5. Cover dish or bowl with foil. Secure tightly with string or a rubber band. Put on rack in pressure pan.
6. Fix lid and bring to pressure. *Allow 35 minutes.*
7. Reduce pressure and remove lid. Lift out dish and remove foil. Sprinkle the top either with crushed potato crisps, cornflakes or fine dry breadcrumbs. If you wish to brown the top, dab on some extra little bits of butter or margarine and brown under the grill or in the oven. Garnish with parsley.

Scalloped potatoes with onions: Put a little grated or finely chopped onion with each layer.

Scalloped potatoes with cheese: Use 3 oz (75 g) grated Cheddar or Parmesan cheese and sprinkle a little with each layer. Save 1 oz for the top and when potatoes are cooked, put under the grill until sizzling.

Scalloped potatoes with bacon: Use 2 or 3 rashers of bacon. Remove rinds and cut bacon into ½ in pieces. Sprinkle one-third with each layer. When cooked, put under the grill to sizzle.

RED CABBAGE, SAVOURY

Time: 20 minutes *Serves 4–6*

1 small or ½ large red cabbage
1 onion, peeled and chopped
1 rasher streaky bacon
2 peeled sliced apples
¼ pint (125 ml) water
3 tablespoons vinegar
2 level tablespoons sugar
salt and pepper
1 clove of garlic, crushed (optional)

1. Wash and cut the cabbage into ¾ in shreds. Prepare onion.
2. Remove rind and cut bacon into 1 in pieces and drop into pressure pan. Fry until fat runs out.
3. Add cabbage, onion, apple, water, vinegar, sugar, salt and pepper. Add garlic, if liked.
4. Fix lid and bring to pressure. *Allow 20 minutes.*
5. Reduce pressure and remove lid. Taste and add more seasoning if necessary.

BLANCHING VEGETABLES FOR THE DEEP FREEZE

Effective and efficient blanching may be done in the pressure pan with only ½ pint (¼ litre) of water and in a matter of seconds. The following is a general guide:

Asparagus, thick: Bring to 5 lb pressure or Low and allow 1 minute. Reduce pressure at once with cold water.

Asparagus, thin: Proceed as for the thicker asparagus, and bring to pressure only, then reduce at once.

Beans, green: Bring to 5 lb pressure or Low and bring to pressure only. Reduce at once.

Beetroot: Bring to 5 lb pressure or Low and allow 5–15 minutes, according to size. Reduce at once.

Broccoli: Bring to 5 lb pressure or Low and bring to pressure only. Reduce at once.

Brussels sprouts: Bring to 5 lb pressure or Low and allow 1 minute. Reduce at once.

Carrots: Bring to 15 lb pressure or High and allow 2 minutes. Reduce at once.

Corn-on-the-cob: Bring to 15 lb pressure or High and allow 2 minutes. Reduce at once.

Peas, fresh: Bring to 5 lb pressure or Low and bring to pressure only. Reduce at once.

5. Fruits, Desserts and Steamed Puddings

Your pressure pan cannot bake you a pie, freeze ice cream or set a jelly! Consequently this chapter has its limitations, but it contains a great variety of desserts, all suited to the talents of a saucepan, especially a pressure pan.

Time-saving benefits are shown particularly in the apple recipes, in the softening of hard pears and stubborn dried fruits such as prunes and apricots; in the delicious 'Baked Custards' plain and caramel and in the steamed puddings, especially the small castle types. See the notes on steamed puddings on *p. 178*.

Using the recipes as a guide, the times could be used for any other dishes you may wish to make or invent. If you wish to increase the ingredients to make more helpings, increase the pressure-cooking times proportionately. As is suggested on *p. 178*, large steamed puddings should not be cooked in a larger bowl, but in smaller containers, either as castles, or in two or three straight-sided tins. When making custards or steamed puddings, take special care that there are no little holes or tears in the foil covering.

STEWED APPLE OR APPLE SAUCE

Time: 2 minutes

For apple sauce or mushy stewed apple, choose cooking apples. For apple compote, where the apples must keep their shape, choose eating ones.

1 lb (½ kg) apples, peeled and sliced
¼ pint (125 ml) water
3 oz (75 g) sugar
grated rind and juice of 1 lemon may be added, in which case add an extra 1 oz (25 g) of sugar
2 or 3 cloves (optional)

1. Put all ingredients into pressure pan.
2. Fix lid and bring to pressure. *Allow 2 minutes.*
3. Reduce pressure and remove lid.

Note: If you wish to use more than 1 lb (½ kg) apples, make sure that the pan is not filled more than half. Apples froth up more than any other food.

Apple shortcake and apple sponge: Follow apricot recipes on *pp. 163* and *165*, using stewed apple instead of apricot.

APPLE SAGO FOAM

Time: 4 minutes *Serves 5–6*

Apple Sago is an old-fashioned sweet that was made by our grandmothers. Today it is brought up to date by the lightness of stiffly beaten egg white. Do not use tapioca as it doesn't dissolve so quickly.

3 level tablespoons small sago
1 lb (½ kg) cooking apples
¼ pint (125 ml) water
½ level teaspoon salt
2 tablespoons golden syrup
grated rind and juice of 1 lemon, or 3 tablespoons lemon juice
2 or 3 egg whites
sugar to taste—4 or more tablespoons, preferably brown

1. Peel and slice the apples and drop into pressure pan. Add sago, water, salt, golden syrup, lemon and sugar. Mix well.
2. Fix lid and bring to pressure. *Allow 4 minutes.*
3. Reduce pressure and remove lid. Pour into a bowl and cool until stiff.
4. Beat the whites of two large or three medium-sized eggs until so stiff that they will not fall from the bowl when it is tipped upside-down. Fold into the apple mixture. Serve with cream, or a pouring custard made with the yolks, ¼ pint (125 ml) milk and 1 level dessertspoon sugar. Do not allow to boil.

APPLE AMBER FLUFF

Time: 2 minutes *Serves 4*

This is a creamy golden-coloured apple sweet, well known in

England for at least a hundred years. In those days the egg yolks only were used and the whites discarded. Today we use the egg whites, stiffly beaten, to lighten the sweet and turn it into a fluff.

1 lb (½ kg) cooking apples
¼ pint (125 ml) water
3 oz (75 g) sugar
grated rind and juice of 1 lemon
2 tablespoons golden syrup
2 level tablespoons custard powder
2 eggs

1. Peel and slice apples. Place in pressure pan. Add water, sugar, lemon and golden syrup.
2. Fix lid and bring to pressure. *Allow 2 minutes.*
3. Reduce pressure and remove lid. Mix custard powder with 3 tablespoons cold water and stir into the apple mixture. Cook until thick and transparent. Remove from heat.
4. Separate the yolks and whites of the eggs, dropping the whites into a fairly large bowl and the yolks into a small one. Beat yolks and stir into the hot apple. Return to heat and cook for 1 minute only. Remove from heat. Allow to cool for about an hour or longer.
5. Beat the whites until very stiff and fold into the apple. Serve cold.

STUFFED APPLES

Time: 3 minutes (see step 4) *Serves 4*

Naturally your pressure-cooked 'baked apples' will not come out tipped with brown, as when oven-cooked, but a few moments under the grill will remedy this. The sago thickens the syrup slightly and dissolves completely.

8 small or 4 large apples
½ pint (¼ litre) hot water
1 rounded teaspoon small sago
3 oz (75 g) brown sugar
2 tablespoons lemon juice
filling of dates and raisins or sultanas or a dried fruit mixture
cinnamon and butter

1. Core the apples, but do not go right through to the other side. Leave the skins on and with a sharp knife cut a line around the circumference, cutting the skin only. This will prevent bursting.

2. Pour the hot water into the pressure pan and add the sago, brown sugar and lemon juice. Boil, uncovered, for 2 minutes.
3. Fill apples with the dried fruit. Sprinkle each with a little cinnamon and top with ½ teaspoon butter.
4. Insert rack and put apples on it. Fix lid and bring to pressure. *Allow 3 minutes.* If the apples are very large they will need an extra minute.
5. Remove pressure pan to a cool surface and allow pressure to reduce gradually. Remove lid. If you wish to tip the apples with brown, put them under grill for about 8 minutes.

Other possible stuffings: Instead of the dried fruit use one of the following: marmalade or jam; ground almonds mixed with sugar and moistened with a liqueur or lemon juice; mixture of coconut, sugar and sultanas—about 3 tablespoons rum could be added to the syrup to give a West Indian touch; honey and dried fruit. Honey could also replace the brown sugar in the syrup.

APPLE BETTY

Time: 15 minutes *Serves 4*

An old English apple pudding that had its name changed to 'Betty' by the American pioneers. From there the name went to the other new countries, Australia and New Zealand. Grated apples and buttered breadcrumbs are layered and flavoured with lemon and spice.

2 rounded tablespoons butter or margarine
4 oz (100 g or 2 cups) fresh brown or white breadcrumbs
2 rounded tablespoons brown sugar
1 level teaspoon mixed spice or cinnamon
1 lb (½ kg) apples, sweet or cooking
2 tablespoons lemon juice and the grated rind of the lemon
3 rounded tablespoons white sugar, 5 if apples are tart

1. Melt the butter or margarine in a small saucepan then tip in the breadcrumbs. Add the brown sugar and spice. Remove from heat. Stir well together.
2. Have ready a dish about 2½ in deep that will fit comfortably in the pressure pan.

F

3. Put ½ cup of the breadcrumb mixture on the bottom of the dish. Grate in half the apples. They may be peeled, or just washed well and left unpeeled.
4. Sprinkle on half the lemon juice and half the white sugar.
5. Spread over ¾ cup of the breadcrumb mixture, then grate on the rest of the apples and sprinkle with the rest of the lemon juice and white sugar. (Save the rest of the breadcrumbs until after pressure-cooking.) Add the grated rind.
6. Pour ½ pint (¼ litre) water into pressure pan and insert rack or trivet. Begin to heat.
7. Cover dish with foil and secure with string or a rubber band. Lower into pressure pan. Fix lid and bring to pressure. *Allow 15 minutes.*
8. Reduce pressure and remove lid. Lift out pudding. Spread with the rest of the breadcrumb mixture and either put into the oven or under the grill to brown and become crisp.

FARMHOUSE APPLE PUDDING

Times: 20 minutes without pressure *Serves 4*
1¼ hours at pressure

An old country English pudding, once known as 'Apple Hat'. A bowl is lined with a special suet crust and filled with sweetened apples. Time saved with pressure-cooking is approximately 1¼ hours.

SUET CRUST
6 oz (150 g) self-raising flour
½ teaspoon salt
1 teaspoon sugar
2 oz (50 g) fresh brown breadcrumbs
2 rounded tablespoons shredded suet
a little water

APPLE FILLING
1 lb (½ kg) apples
3 oz (75 g) sugar or to taste
¼ pint (125 ml) water (the juice of half a lemon could replace some of the water, in which case add an extra tablespoon sugar)

1. Sieve flour and salt into mixing bowl. Add sugar, breadcrumbs and suet. Mix to a soft dough with a little water.
2. Cut off a quarter of the dough for the lid. Roll the rest out to

about ⅛ in thickness and line a greased pudding bowl. Cut around to neaten.

3. Fill with the peeled, sliced apple and add sugar and water. Add also the lemon juice if used.
4. Put 1½ pints (¾ litre) water into pressure pan and insert rack. Begin to heat.
5. Add trimmings of dough to the extra piece and roll out. Cover bowl with it and press around to seal. Cover with foil and secure with string or a rubber band. Lower into pressure pan and fix lid.
6. Steam without pressure for 20 minutes, then close vent and bring to pressure. *Allow 1¼ hours.*
7. Move to a cool surface and let pressure reduce gradually. Remove lid. Lift out pudding and remove foil. Either turn out or serve from the bowl.

APRICOTS, DRIED

Time: 12 minutes

Ripe soft apricots should not be pressure-cooked. They only take a few minutes to stew. To 1 lb (½ kg) dried apricots allow 2 pints (1 litre) water and ¾ lb (300 g) sugar. Part orange juice may be used.

1. Put apricots, liquid and sugar into pressure pan.
2. Fix lid and bring to pressure. *Allow 12 minutes.*
3. Reduce pressure and remove lid.

Mixed dried fruits (apricots, pears, peaches, prunes and apples): Cooked in the same way. Less sugar may be used.

APRICOT SHORTCAKE

Times: 12 minutes for apricots *Serves 5–6*
35–40 minutes for shortcake, in the oven

Pressure-cooked mashed dried apricots are sandwiched between two layers of shortcake pastry. Delicious eaten either hot or cold.

FILLING

6 oz (150 g) dried apricots
1 pint (½ litre) water, or part water and part orange juice
6 oz (150 g) sugar

SHORTCAKE

4 oz (100 g) butter or margarine
4 oz (100 g) sugar
8 oz (200 g) self-raising flour
1 egg
¼ teaspoon salt

1. Put apricots, liquid and sugar into pressure pan. Fix lid and bring to pressure. *Allow 12 minutes.* Reduce pressure and remove lid. Tip apricots into a bowl. Mash.
2. For the shortcake, cream the butter or margarine with the sugar. Add 1 tablespoon of the flour and mix in. Add the unbeaten egg and mix until smooth.
3. Add the rest of the flour with the salt. Form into a soft dough and divide into two pieces. Roll each piece out to fit a greased 8 in or 8½ in cake pan, about 1 in deep.
4. Line the pan with one piece.
5. Drain off some of the syrup from the apricots if the mixture seems wet. Spread it on the pastry. Cover with the other piece of rolled-out pastry. Pinch the edges to seal and prick the top here and there with a fork.
6. Bake in a moderate oven, 350 °F or gas mark 4, for 35–40 minutes. Leave in the pan until cool. Dust with icing sugar.

APRICOT CHIFFON PIE

Times: 12 minutes for apricots
about 20 minutes for pastry, in the oven

Serves 5–6

4 oz (100 g) dried apricots
½ pint (¼ litre) water
6 oz (150 g) sugar
1 level tablespoon cornflour or custard powder
¼ teaspoon salt
3 level teaspoons powdered gelatine
4 tablespoons cream or evaporated milk
2 tablespoons Apricot Brandy (optional)
2 egg whites (see Note)
6 oz (150 g) short pastry or Crumb Crust (see following recipe)

1. Put washed apricots, water and sugar into pressure pan. Fix lid and bring to pressure. *Allow 12 minutes.*
2. Reduce pressure and remove lid. Mix cornflour with 3 tablespoons cold water and salt, and stir in. Cook without pressure until syrup has thickened slightly and is clear and smooth.

3. Mix gelatine with 2 tablespoons cold water and stir into the hot apricot mixture. Allow to dissolve completely. Pour into a bowl and set aside in a cold place until just beginning to set. Stir in the cream, or evaporated milk, and, for a special occasion, the Apricot Brandy (*see Note*).
4. Meanwhile make the pastry (your usual recipe) and line a greased 8 in or 9 in dish about 1½ in deep. Neaten the edge and decorate it. Put a few pieces of stale bread on the bottom to prevent the pastry from rising. Bake for about 20 minutes in a moderate oven until lightly browned. Or make the Crumb Crust from the recipe which follows.
5. Whisk the apricot mixture to break up the fruit. Beat the egg whites until very stiff and fold in.
6. When pie crust is cold pour the mixture in and allow to set. Top with whipped cream.

Note: If the evaporated milk contains no fat, the apricot mixture may be beaten with an electric mixer without any egg whites. Whisk until the mixture almost doubles in bulk and becomes very light and fluffy. This is not possible where there are cream, egg yolks or any fat.

Crumb crust: Crush 4 oz (100 g) sweet biscuits (half digestive) either with a rolling-pin or in electric blender. Tip into a bowl and add 2 oz (50 g) light brown sugar, 2½ level tablespoons melted butter and ½ teaspoon vanilla essence. Mix until crumbs are moist. Line the dish with mixture, pressing it over bottom and sides. Don't bother to neaten it at this stage. Put away in refrigerator and when firm it will be easier to manage. Neaten the edge. Pour in the filling and leave until set. Top with whipped cream.

APRICOT SPONGE

Times: 12 minutes for dried apricots
40–45 minutes in the oven

Serves 4–6

A fruit pudding with a sponge on top.

½ lb (¼ kg) dried apricots or dried mixed fruits (see p. 163)

1 pint (½ litre) water, or part water and part orange juice

2 or 3 tablespoons lemon juice may be added instead of or as well as the orange juice

8 oz (200 g) sugar or to taste

sponge mixture (see following recipe)

1. In the pressure pan cook the apricots or dried fruits, water and sugar, *allowing 12 minutes* at pressure.
2. Meanwhile, preheat oven to 350 °F or gas mark 4. Make a one-egg mixture sponge, as in the following recipe.
3. When the time is up, reduce pressure and remove lid. Tip fruit into a deep ovenproof dish and while still boiling hot, pour the sponge mixture on top.
4. Bake for 40–45 minutes. When cooked, dust with icing sugar.

One-egg sponge: Whisk together 1 egg and 4 oz (100 g) sugar. In a small saucepan melt 1 tablespoon butter and 3 tablespoons water. To the egg and sugar add 5½ oz (138 g) self-raising flour and ½ teaspoon salt, adding it alternately with the melted mixture.

FIGS, DRIED

Time: 10 minutes

1 lb (½ kg) dried figs
1 pint (½ litre) water
4 oz (100 g) sugar
3 level teaspoons small sago (not tapioca)
4 tablespoons lemon juice

1. Put figs into pressure pan and add water, sugar, sago and lemon juice.
2. Fix lid and bring to pressure. *Allow 10 minutes.* About 3 or 4 tablespoons chopped preserved ginger may be added.

PEARS

Times: 2 minutes for firm ripe pears
5–7 minutes for hard ones

(Do not pressure-cook soft ripe pears.)

1. Peel, halve and core the pears and put into pressure pan.
2. To 1 lb (½ kg) allow ½ pint (¼ litre) water, 2 level teaspoons small

sago (this may be omitted, but it does give a little body to the syrup), and 2 oz (50 g) sugar.

3. Lemon is often added, allow the juice of half and increase the sugar by another 1 oz (25 g).
4. Fix lid and bring to pressure. *Allow times shown above.*
5. Reduce pressure and remove lid.

Pears with syrup and ginger: Follow directions for cooking pears but replace ¼ cup of the water and 2 oz (50 g) of the sugar with 2 good tablespoons golden syrup. Lemon may still be included and will still need the extra 2 oz (50 g) sugar. Lastly add 2 tablespoons chopped preserved ginger.

Marshmallow pears: Halve and core the pears, then pressure-cook as directed. When lid has been removed, lift out pears with a slotted spoon and place them on the grilling rack. Put a marshmallow in the hollow of each and grill until they begin to melt and are tinged with gold. Do not allow them to burn.

Toasted coconut pears: Halve and core the pears and pressure-cook as directed. When lid has been removed, lift pears out with a slotted spoon and place on grilling rack. Fill hollows with chopped raisins and walnuts, then sprinkle generously with coconut. Grill gently until coconut is golden. It burns very easily, so watch it.

To the syrup left in the pressure pan, add a little cochineal to make the syrup a pale pink, then thicken with 2 teaspoons arrowroot mixed with a little water. Cook until clear and slightly thick. Place the pears in a serving dish and pour the syrup around, but not over them.

Pears with toasted almond: Halve and core the pears and pressure-cook as directed. When lid has been removed, lift pears out with a slotted spoon and place on grilling rack.

Make a mixture of 2 oz (50 g) ground almonds, 2 tablespoons sherry, ½ teaspoon almond essence and 3 tablespoons sugar. Fill hollows of pears with this, then put under grill until lightly browned. **Peaches** may be served in any of these pear variations.

PEACHES

Times: 5 minutes for whole unripe peaches
3 minutes for halved unripe ones

(Do not pressure-cook soft ripe peaches.)

1. To 1 lb (½ kg) unripe peaches allow ½ pint (¼ litre) water, 1 tablespoon lemon juice and about 3 oz (75 g) sugar.
2. Instead of peeling, they could be rubbed all over with a pot scourer (not the metal kind). If large, they should be halved and the stone removed.
3. Put everything into the pressure pan. Fix lid and bring to pressure. *Allow times shown above.*
4. Reduce pressure and remove lid.

Note: For variations see pear recipes.

PLUMS

Time: 2 minutes for hard plums

(Do not pressure-cook soft plums.)

1. For each 1 lb (½ kg) unripe plums add ¼ pint (125 ml) water and 4–6 oz (100–150 g) sugar, depending on tartness.
2. Fix lid and bring to pressure. *Allow 2 minutes.*
3. Reduce pressure and remove lid.

PRUNES

Time: 12 minutes

To 1 lb (½ kg) washed prunes allow 1½ pints (¾ litre) water, 3 oz (75 g) sugar and 1 level tablespoon small sago (not tapioca). The juice and grated rind of 1 lemon may be added, in which case increase sugar to 5 oz (125 g). Put everything into pressure pan, fix lid and bring to pressure and *allow 12 minutes.* Reduce pressure and remove lid.

Prunes with coffee or tea: Cook prunes as directed, using part strong coffee or tea and part water. When using coffee, add ½ teaspoon vanilla essence and when using tea, add ½ level teaspoon cinnamon.

PRUNE FLUFF

Time: 12 minutes *Serves 4–6*

Instead of serving the prunes as they are, turn them into this light airy sweet.

½ lb (200 g) prunes
5 oz (125 g) sugar
grated rind and juice of 1 lemon
1 pint (½ litre) water
½ teaspoon salt
1 level tablespoon powdered gelatine
whites of 2 eggs
chopped walnuts

1. Wash the prunes and put into pressure pan with the sugar, lemon, water, and salt.
2. Fix lid and bring to pressure. *Allow 12 minutes.*
3. Reduce pressure and remove lid. Tip prunes into a bowl and when cool enough to handle, lift them out with a slotted spoon and remove the stones.
4. Measure syrup and bring up to 1 pint (½ litre) with water if necessary. Return syrup to pan. Add prunes.
5. Mix gelatine with 4 tablespoons cold water and stir in. Heat and stir until gelatine has dissolved. Tip into a large bowl and set aside until beginning to thicken.
6. If you have an electric mixer, whisk the jelly, adding the unbeaten egg whites. Continue whisking until it almost doubles. If you have no electric mixer, beat the egg whites until very stiff, then fold into the half-set jelly.
7. Tip into a serving dish and allow to set. Sprinkle with chopped walnuts and serve with cream.

RHUBARB

Times: 2 minutes (garden)
1 minute (forced)

1. Wash rhubarb and cut into 1½ in pieces. Drop into pressure pan.
2. For each 1 lb (½ kg) of rhubarb allow ¼ pint (125 ml) water and 6 oz (150 g) or more of sugar.

3. Fix lid and bring to pressure. *Allow above times.* Reduce pressure at once and remove lid.

RHUBARB WITH DATES

Times: 2 minutes (garden)
1 minute (forced)

Serves 4

1 lb (½ kg) rhubarb
4 oz (100 g) dates stoned
6 oz (150 g) sugar
¼ pint (125 ml) water
¼ teaspoon salt
½ teaspoon vanilla essence

1. Wash the rhubarb and cut into 1½ in pieces. Drop into pressure pan.
2. Add the dates, sugar, water, salt and vanilla. Fix lid and bring to pressure. *Allow above times.*
3. Reduce pressure and remove lid.

FRUIT FOOL

Serves 4–6

Cook any fruit as directed, remove stones where necessary, and purée in a sieve or electric blender. Mix with an equal quantity of thick custard and thick cream and chill. For a foamy result, fold in two stiffly beaten egg whites.

EGG CUSTARD (small)

Time: 5 minutes

Serves 2–3

Save all that oven heat by cooking 'Baked Custards' economically in a pressure pan.

½ pint plus 2 tablespoons (281 ml) heated milk
2 large or 3 small eggs
1 level tablespoon sugar
½ teaspoon vanilla essence or flavouring from a pod
pinch of salt
nutmeg

1. Have ready a soufflé dish or other container that can be brought to the table, and will fit easily into the pressure pan. The size could be 6–6½ in across and 2–2½ in deep.

2. Put ½ pint (¼ litre) of water into pressure pan and insert rack or trivet. Begin to heat.
3. Heat the milk. If you are using a pod infuse it in the milk. Do not heat to boiling.
4. Beat the eggs with the sugar, salt and vanilla in the dish. It will save washing up. Add the milk (remove the pod), and stir well.
5. Cover dish with foil and secure with string or a rubber band. Lower into pressure pan. Fix lid and bring to pressure. *Allow 5 minutes.*
6. Move pan to a cool surface and let the pressure reduce gradually. Remove lid.
7. Lift out the custard and sprinkle with nutmeg. Allow to cool before serving.

Egg custard (Larger size. *Serves 4–5*): Use 3 large eggs, ¾ pint (375 ml) milk and 1½ level tablespoons sugar. *Allow 7 minutes.*

Almond egg custard: Add 1 tablespoon ground almonds and ½ teaspoon almond essence. A little brandy may be added.

Chocolate egg custard: Add 1 tablespoon grated chocolate.

Coconut egg custard: Add 1 tablespoon desiccated coconut.

Coffee egg custard: Add 1 heaped teaspoon instant coffee.

CARAMEL CUSTARD

Time: 8 minutes *Serves 4*

Again we save oven heat and produce 'Baked Custards' that are smooth and firm in a matter of minutes.

3 rounded tablespoons sugar and 2 tablespoons water, for caramel
¾ pint (375 ml) milk
3 large eggs
2 level tablespoons sugar
pinch of salt
¼ teaspoon vanilla essence or flavouring from a pod

1. Prepare a dish as in the preceding recipe.
2. To make the caramel, boil together in a small saucepan with a

thick base the 3 tablespoons sugar and 2 of water. When the syrup turns a golden colour remove from heat and pour into the dish in which the custard is to be cooked: don't worry if it turns instantly into toffee.

3. Put ½ pint (¼ litre) water into pressure pan and insert rack or trivet. Begin to heat.
4. Heat the milk. If you are using a vanilla pod, infuse it in the milk. Do not heat to boiling-point.
5. Beat the eggs in a bowl and add the sugar, salt, vanilla and the warm milk. Remove the pod, if used.
6. Pour into dish on top of caramel. Cover with foil and secure with string or a rubber band. Lower into pressure pan.
7. Fix lid and bring to pressure. *Allow 8 minutes.*
8. Remove pan to a cool surface and let the pressure reduce gradually. Remove lid.
9. Lift out the custard and allow to cool. Turn out.

Caramel custards (individual): Follow preceding recipe, using 4 teacup-sized containers or 8 smaller ones and pouring a little caramel into each container. Cover each with a small square of foil.

Fix lid, *allow 3 minutes*, then let the pressure reduce gradually.

Note: The little custards could be stacked in the pressure pan. Put some into the pan without the rack, then cover with the rack and put the rest on top. Another idea is to cover the lower custards with two thicknesses of foil instead of the rack and put the rest on top.

PEARS WITH CUSTARD

Time: 5 minutes *Serves 3–4*

The custard and pears together will take 5 minutes, so if the pears are the very green hard kind, it would be wise to cut them in quarters instead of halves. But the average unripe pear will cook successfully in the 5 minutes, even if only in halves.

1 lb (½ kg) pears, peeled, halved and cored
½ pint (¼ litre) water
2 oz (50 g) sugar
juice of half a lemon could be added, and if so increase sugar to 4 oz (100 g)

CUSTARD

½ pint (¼ litre) milk
2 large eggs
2 level tablespoons sugar
½ teaspoon vanilla essence or flavouring from a pod

1. Put pears, water and sugar into pressure pan. Add lemon and extra sugar if liked. Begin to heat.
2. Heat milk and add vanilla or pod.
3. Beat eggs with the sugar, then stir into milk (remove the pod). Mix well. Have ready a bowl or soufflé dish that will fit comfortably into pressure pan. Grease it lightly. Pour in the custard mixture. Cover with foil.
4. Put into pressure pan on top of pears. Fix lid and bring to pressure. *Allow 5 minutes.*
5. Remove pan to a cool surface and let pressure reduce gradually. Remove lid.

Note: Any of the other flavoured custards on *p. 171* would be delicious with the pears.

RICE CUSTARD

Time: 12 minutes *Serves 4*

A nicely set Rice Custard may be made in your pressure saucepan. With cooked fruit it makes a favourite dessert.

2 large or 3 small eggs
2 level tablespoons sugar (*or more if you wish*)
½ pint (*¼ litre*) *milk, heated*
8 oz (*¼ kg or 1¼ cups*) *cooked rice* (p. 198)
½ teaspoon vanilla essence
sultanas may be added, about 2–3 tablespoons

1. Have ready a dish that will fit comfortably in the pressure pan and which can be brought to the table. In this dish beat the eggs and sugar.
2. Heat milk in a small saucepan.
3. Pour ½ pint (¼ litre) water into pressure pan and insert rack. Begin to heat.
4. Add rice, milk and vanilla to eggs and sugar. Add the sultanas if liked. Mix well.

5. Cover dish with foil and secure with string or a rubber band.
6. Lower into pressure pan and fix lid. Bring to pressure and *allow 12 minutes.*
7. Move pan to a cool surface and let the pressure reduce gradually.

QUICK QUEEN'S PUDDING

Time: 10 minutes *Serves 4*

The traditional Queen of Puddings has a bread and jam custard base with a meringue topping. This topping cannot be done in the pressure pan, but must be crisped in the oven.

6 slices, about ¼ in thick, from a large loaf
butter and jam or marmalade
2 large eggs or 3 small, separated
1 level tablespoon sugar
¾ pint (375 ml) milk
4 oz (100 g) sugar for the meringue and a pinch of salt

1. Remove crusts from bread, if you wish, and spread slices with butter and jam. Cut each slice into three.
2. Have ready a heat-proof bowl that will fit comfortably in the pressure pan, about 6½ in across by 4 in deep, or 7 in across and 3 in deep.
3. Arrange the bread in the bowl.
4. Beat the yolks with the sugar and add the milk. Pour over the bread. Cover with foil and secure with string or a rubber band.
5. Pour 1 pint (½ litre) water into pressure pan and insert rack or trivet. Lower bowl into pan. Fix lid and bring to pressure. *Allow 10 minutes.*
6. Meanwhile bring oven to 250 °F or gas mark 2½.
7. When time is up, reduce pressure and remove lid. The custard will cook a little more in the oven. Remove the foil.
8. Beat the egg whites with the salt until *very* stiff, then gently fold in the sugar. If you have an electric mixer, the eggs and sugar could be beaten together until very stiff.
9. Pile meringue on top of the pudding and bake in the oven for about 20 minutes, or until meringue is crisp on the outside.

CABINET PUDDING

Time: 12 minutes *Serves 4*

As this is a colourful pudding, it would look attractive in a heat-proof glass dish. It has been made in England for so many generations that it has long since earned the title of 'traditional'.

a single 7 in sponge round
¼ pint (125 ml) sherry
about 4 oz (100 g) mixed crystallised fruits such as cherries, orange and lemon segments and pieces of angelica or sliced green jujubes
2 medium-sized eggs
½ pint (250 ml) milk, heated
1 level tablespoon sugar
½ teaspoon vanilla essence or a pod

1. Have ready a heat-proof glass soufflé dish that will fit comfortably in the pressure pan. It need not be greased.
2. Break the sponge into pieces and put half in the dish. Pour over them half the sherry.
3. Cut the cherries in halves and cut the other fruits into small pieces. Spread over the cake, using them all.
4. Add the rest of the cake and sherry.
5. Pour ½ pint (¼ litre) water into the pressure pan and insert rack or trivet. Begin to heat.
6. Beat the eggs with the milk, sugar and vanilla essence. If you are using the pod infuse it in the milk first, then remove. Pour the mixture over the cake. Cover dish with foil and secure with a rubber band or string. Lower into pressure pan.
7. Fix lid and bring to pressure. *Allow 12 minutes.*
8. Move pan to a cool surface and let the pressure reduce gradually. Remove lid and lift out pudding.
9. Allow to cool and serve piled with whipped cream. Decorate with a few crystallised fruits.

BREAD PUDDING WITH JAM AND SHERRY

Time: 15 minutes *Serves 4*

Stale bread, crusts and all, may be quickly turned into a pudding that will entice the family to ask for more. After pressure-cooking, the top is sprinkled with coconut then toasted until brown under the grill.

5 slices from a large cut loaf
butter and jam
2 eggs, medium or large
3 tablespoons sherry
¾ pint (375 ml) milk, warmed
2 level tablespoons sugar
coconut

1. Have ready a heat-proof dish, about 6½ in across and 2 in deep, that will fit comfortably in the pressure pan.
2. Spread the slices with butter and jam and cut each into halves crosswise. Place, jam upwards, overlapping in the dish. Pour the sherry over.
3. Beat the eggs in a bowl and add the milk and sugar. Mix well and pour over the bread.
4. Put ½ pint (250 ml) water into pressure pan and begin to heat. Insert rack or trivet.
5. Cover dish with foil and secure with a rubber band. Lower into pressure pan.
6. Fix lid and bring to pressure. *Allow 15 minutes.*
7. Reduce pressure at once and remove lid. Lift out pudding and remove foil. Sprinkle the top generously with coconut, then put under a hot grill for a few moments until coconut has browned. Keep an eye on it as it burns easily.

PINEAPPLE AND CHERRY PRETTY PUDDING

Time: 15 minutes pressure cooking *Serves 4–5*

Easy, attractive, quick and economical. Take special note of this recipe when the bread-bin contains left-overs, and give them a worthy last appearance.

4 slices of white bread about ¼ in thick
15½ oz (430 g) can of pineapple in cubes or pieces
2 tablespoons glacé cherries, halved
¼ pint (125 ml) milk
2 eggs, medium or large
2 level tablespoons sugar
¼ teaspoon salt

1. Have ready a bowl or soufflé dish that will fit into the pressure pan. Grease it well.
2. Cut bread into 1½ in squares and put 4 or 5 into the bowl or dish.
3. Open can of pineapple. Tip syrup into a small jug and pour a quarter of it over the bread.
4. Add one-third of the pineapple. If in cubes, halve them. Sprinkle in one-third of the cherries.
5. Repeat with the bread, syrup, pineapple and cherries until all are used up.
6. Pour ¾ pint (375 ml) water into pressure pan and insert rack or trivet. Begin to heat.
7. Warm the milk. Beat the eggs and sugar, then stir in the milk and salt. Mix well and pour over the ingredients in the bowl. Let it stand for a few minutes until bread has been soaked. Cover with a piece of foil, pressing it well around the sides. Lower into pressure pan.
8. Fix lid and bring to pressure. *Allow 15 minutes.* Remove pressure pan to a cool surface and let the pressure reduce gradually. Remove lid.
9. Lift out pudding and remove foil. Allow pudding to stand for 10 minutes before serving, or serve cold.

FRUIT-CAKE PUDDING

Time: 15 minutes *Serves 3–4*

If you have some left-over fruit-cake, salve your conscience by turning it into an appetising pudding. Plain cake or gingerbread could be used instead.

about 8 oz (200 g) stale fruit cake
4 tablespoons sherry or other wine
1 large or 2 small eggs
1 level tablespoon sugar
¼ pint (125 ml) milk
½ teaspoon salt

1. Have ready a pudding bowl, about 3½–4 in deep and 5½–6 in across.
2. Crumble the cake into it and pour the wine over.
3. Pour ½ pint (¼ litre) water into pressure pan. Begin to heat.
4. Beat the egg in a bowl and add the sugar, milk and salt. Stir well, then pour over the cake crumbs.

5. Cover with foil and secure with a rubber band or string. Lower into pressure pan.
6. Fix lid and bring to pressure. *Allow 15 minutes.*
7. Reduce pressure and remove lid.

Steamed Puddings

Large single steamed puddings (like large pieces of meat) do not pressure-cook well, and for this reason only medium- and small-sized steamed puddings are included. The small individual castle puddings are particularly light.

In one pudding bowl: To be successful puddings should not be large and need either 5 lb (low pressure), or as in the Christmas pudding 10 lb (medium pressure). When using the Prestige cooker, choose the small weight and when using the Presto, bring pressure to the first white ring for low and the second one for medium.

Small individual castle puddings: These are the most successful of all pressure-cooked steamed puddings. The 15 lb (high pressure) may be maintained and the cooking times are very short. They emerge light and well risen.

Twin-tin puddings: A larger mixture with many more servings may be cooked in two straight-sided tins side by side. For the average-sized pressure pan, use tins about 3½–4 in across (depending on the width of the pan) and 4–4½ in deep. For still larger quantities, tins 5 in deep may be used as all pressure pan lids are higher at the point of the vent and this would allow room for the steam to circulate. High-dome pans will take even deeper tins.

Triple-tin puddings: If you have tins that have held some sort of canned food, and which have straight sides with smooth edges, they may also be used for pressure-cooked steamed puddings. They should be approximately 3 in across and 4–4½ in deep. They would hold larger mixtures and would need only 18 minutes instead of 25. Use the 10 lb (medium pressure).

Rising: Although pressure-cooked steamed puddings will rise, those cooked without pressure will rise a little higher but need twice the cooking time and so use much more fuel. The choice is yours.

STEAMED SPONGE PUDDING, BASIC RECIPE

Time: 20 minutes without pressure — *Serves 4*
25 minutes at 5 lb pressure (low)
(see step 1)

No matter how big your pressure cooker may be, this is the largest sized steamed pudding it will cook satisfactorily in one bowl.

2½ oz (63 g) butter or margarine
3 rounded tablespoons sugar (preferably castor)
5½ oz (138 g) self-raising flour
1 large or 2 small eggs
½ teaspoon salt
5 tablespoons milk or milk and water
½ teaspoon vanilla essence

1. Have ready a greased 1½ pint (¾ litre) pudding bowl, preferably metal or heat-proof plastic. If it is thick glass or china allow 28 minutes instead of 25. Grease it well.
2. Cream butter or margarine and sugar, adding 2 teaspoons boiling or very hot water to help it along. Use your electric mixer if you have one.
3. Add 1 tablespoon of the flour, then add the egg or eggs, and beat well until light and smooth.
4. Sieve in the rest of the flour alternately with the liquid, adding the salt and vanilla essence. Mix well.
5. Put 1 pint (½ litre) water into pressure pan. Insert rack or trivet. Begin to heat.
6. Tip mixture into bowl. Cover with foil and secure tightly with string or a rubber band. Lower into pressure pan.
7. Fix lid and let the water boil gently under the bowl without pressure for 20 minutes.
8. Now put on the weight and bring only to 5 lb pressure (low). *Allow 25 minutes.* Try to keep the pressure constant.

9. Move pan to a cool surface and let the pressure reduce gradually. Remove lid and lift out pudding. Take off the foil and turn out.

Chocolate steamed sponge pudding: Use 1 rounded teaspoon cocoa with the flour and increase vanilla to 1 teaspoon.

Coffee steamed sponge pudding: Replace the liquid with strong coffee or add 1 heaped teaspoon of instant coffee to the flour.

Mocha steamed sponge pudding: Add 1 heaped teaspoon cocoa to the flour and either replace the milk with strong coffee or add 1 heaped teaspoon of instant coffee.

Canary steamed sponge pudding: Replace the liquid with lemon juice and the grated rind. Increase sugar by 1 level tablespoon. The vanilla blends well with the lemon.

Sultana steamed sponge pudding: Use any of the variations and add 3 oz (75 g or ⅓ cup) sultanas. *Increase pressure-cooking time to 28 minutes.*

Jam-topped steamed sponge pudding: Put 2 or 3 tablespoons jam or marmalade into the greased bowl. A dark jam would turn it into a Black Cap Pudding. When the pudding is turned out, the jam will be at the top and should fall around the pudding.

STEAMED CASTLE PUDDINGS

Times: 5 minutes without pressure *Serves 4*
15 minutes at 15 lb pressure (high)

Small individual puddings will be lighter than one large one.

1. For 4 containers, each a little over ¼ pint size (125 ml), either use the recipe for Steamed Sponge Pudding (*p. 179*) or the 1 egg sponge cake recipe (*p. 166*).
2. Have ready greased containers that will fit comfortably in the pressure pan. They could be teacups without handles, ¼ pint (125 ml) moulds, narrow coffee cups, small tins that have held

coffee or other canned foods, or beakers. If using thick pottery containers allow 2 minutes longer at pressure.

3. Make the sponge mixture as suggested. Put into the containers.
4. Pour ½ pint (¼ litre) water into pressure pan and insert rack or trivet. Begin to heat.
5. Cover containers with 4 in squares of foil and secure with rubber bands. Lower into pressure pan. Fix lid and let the water boil for 5 minutes.
6. Close vent and bring to pressure. *Allow 15 minutes.*
7. Move pan to a cool surface and let the pressure reduce gradually. Remove lid. Take out puddings, remove foil and turn out.

Variations: Any of the variations suggested after first basic recipe on *p. 180*, may be used for the Castle Puddings.

STEAMED DUSKY DATE PUDDING

Time: 20 minutes without pressure *Serves 4–5*
30 minutes at 5 lb pressure (low)

This is cooked in one bowl, but more time could be saved by cooking the mixture in small containers as with Castle Puddings in the preceding recipe.

3 oz (75 g) dates, chopped
4 tablespoons lemon juice or water (or half and half)
3 rounded tablespoons brown sugar
2 oz (50 g) butter or margarine
2 standard eggs
6 oz (150 g or 1 cup) self-raising flour
½ teaspoon salt
4 tablespoons milk
½ teaspoon vanilla essence
½ teaspoon cinnamon (optional)

1. Grease well a 1½ pint (¾ litre) pudding bowl.
2. Put the dates and lemon juice or water into a small saucepan and bring to the boil. Remove from heat and mash. Tip into a mixing bowl. Add the sugar.
3. Add the butter or margarine and stir until mixed in. Add the eggs and beat well.
4. Sieve in the flour and salt alternately with the milk, adding the vanilla and cinnamon if liked. Mix well and tip into the greased bowl.

5. Put 1 pint (½ litre) water into pressure pan and insert rack. Begin to heat.
6. Cover bowl with foil. Tie with string or secure with a rubber band. Lower into pressure pan.
7. Fix lid and let water boil gently underneath. Cook without pressure for 20 minutes.
8. Close vent and bring to 5 lb pressure (low). Keep it that way and *allow 30 minutes.*
9. Move pan to a cool surface and let the pressure reduce gradually. Remove lid, lift out pudding, take off the foil and turn out.

CHRISTMAS PUDDINGS, TWIN-TINS

Time in two tins: 25 minutes without pressure
2 hours at 10 lb pressure (medium)
Serves 7–8

By using the two tins as suggested on *p. 178* one can double the pudding servings while still keeping to the rule that large single puddings do not pressure-cook well. The twin puddings are delicious and cook in half the time.

6 oz (150 g or 3 cups) breadcrumbs
6 oz (150 g) self-raising flour
4 oz (100 g) suet
6 oz (150 g) brown sugar
6 oz (150 g) sultanas
4 oz (100 g) raisins
3 oz (75 g) currants
2 oz (50 g) glacé cherries
2 oz (50 g) chopped mixed peel
2 oz (50 g) blanched sliced almonds
2 standard eggs
1 good tablespoon golden syrup or treacle
¼ pint (125 ml) beer or milk
½ teaspoon salt
1 level teaspoon mixed spice
½ teaspoon each vanilla, lemon and almond essences
1 level teaspoon bicarbonate of soda dissolved in 1 tablespoon water

1. Have ready two well-greased straight-sided tins of about 1½ pints (¾ litre) size. See *Note* at end of recipe. Make sure that they will sit side by side.
2. Put breadcrumbs, flour, suet and sugar into a mixing bowl.
3. In another bowl beat the eggs with the syrup until light and frothy. Add beer or milk. Stir into dry ingredients, adding the salt and spice.

4. Add the cleaned fruits and the essences, then the bicarbonate of soda and water. Mix well.
5. Put 2½ pints (1¼ litre) water into pressure pan and begin to heat. Insert rack.
6. If the tins have tight fitting lids, put a round of foil or greaseproof paper on the top of them before fixing the lids, which will make them even tighter. If they have no lids cover closely with foil, pressing all around, and tie tightly with string. Lower into pressure pan.
7. Fix lid and let the water boil gently for 25 minutes without pressure.
8. Close vent and bring to 10 lb pressure (medium).
9. Lower heat and *allow 2 hours.* Try to keep the pressure constant.
10. When the time is up, let the pressure reduce gradually. When pressure is absolutely normal, remove weight and lid. Turn the puddings out. If they have been made in advance, wrap in greaseproof paper and store.
11. To reheat, remove paper, put puddings back into tins and place on rack in pressure pan. Pour in ¼ pint (125 ml) water. Bring to pressure and *allow 10 minutes.* Let pressure reduce gradually. Serve with Brandy Sauce (*p. 194*), Brandy Butter (*p. 194*) or Hard Sauce (*p. 194*).

Note: 3½–4 in wide, 4–4½ in deep tins would be ideal for this quantity. For the smaller 1¼ pint size, reduce the mixture thus: use 4 oz (100 g) breadcrumbs, 4 oz (100 g) self-raising flour, 5 oz (125 g) sugar and 4 oz (100 g) sultanas. Reduce liquid by 1 tablespoon. *Allow 1¾ hours* at 10 lb pressure (medium).

Small Christmas pudding in one bowl: To make a small pudding to serve 4–5 people, make half the quantity given in the main recipe. Tip mixture into a well-greased 1½ pint (¾ litre) bowl. Cover as suggested in the recipe and *allow the same time.*

Small Christmas puddings in two tins: Use two tins about 3 in across and 4½ in deep. Grease well. Make half the quantity given in the main recipe. Cover securely with foil and tie with string or use a rubber band. *Allow 10 minutes* without pressure then put on weight, bring to 15 lb pressure (high) and *allow 1 hour.*

6. Cakes: Steam-Cooked in the Pressure Pan

Mixtures that depend on the lightness given by eggs and baking powder do not respond well to very high temperatures, so the following cakes are steam-cooked in the pressure pan, but *without pressure.*

In bedsits, very small flats and boats and caravans this method can be a blessing. Without an oven, delicious cakes can be produced. The mixture is put into the cake tin, covered closely with foil, and put on to the rack in the pressure pan. Water boils gently underneath and an enamel plate replaces the cooker lid. When time is up, the tin is removed, the foil lifted off and a perfect evenly risen cake is revealed. A reliable timer is very useful for cake-making.

Because the temperature of the boiling water under the cake is less than in an oven, times are a little longer, but in spite of this, fuel costs are less. No preheating is necessary as in the oven, and the water can be kept gently boiling on a very low heat. Perhaps when you have tried the recipes you will adopt this simple method permanently, even if you have an oven. Of two things you can be certain. Your cakes will not burn, nor will they be dry!

Remember to put a little vinegar or lemon juice in the water (*see p. 17*), and make absolutely certain that there are no little holes or tears in the foil covering.

COCONUT MARMALADE GINGERBREAD

Time: 1 hour 40 minutes *Yield: about 1¼ lb (600 g)*

A gingerbread that is light and moist.

3 oz (75 g) butter or margarine
2 tablespoons golden syrup
2 tablespoons marmalade
7 oz (175 g) self-raising flour

½ teaspoon salt
3 level teaspoons ground ginger
2 rounded tablespoons desiccated coconut
2 rounded tablespoons brown sugar
1 large or 2 small eggs
2 tablespoons milk
½ teaspoon vanilla essence

1. Have ready a cake tin about 6–6½ in across and 2½ in deep, or a small loaf pan if it will fit the pressure pan. Grease well, if not non-stick.
2. In a small saucepan melt the butter or margarine, the golden syrup and the marmalade. Remove from heat.
3. Sieve the flour, salt and ginger into a mixing bowl. Add coconut and sugar.
4. Pour 1½ pints (¾ litre) water into pressure pan. Insert rack and begin to heat.
5. Beat the egg in a small bowl and add the milk and vanilla. Stir into melted mixture. Add this to dry ingredients and mix well. Tip into the cake or loaf tin. Cover with foil and secure firmly with string or a rubber band.
6. Lower into pressure pan. Cover with an enamel plate. Let water boil gently and allow the cake to steam for *1 hour and 40 minutes.*
7. Lift out the tin, remove foil, and turn the cake out after about 5 minutes.

DATE AND WALNUT CAKE

Time: 1 hour 40 minutes *Yield: 1 lb 6 oz (650 g)*

The dates are mashed first and so merge all through the cake to give a rich colour and flavour. The walnuts provide the crunch.

4 oz (100 g) stoned dates
2 tablespoons lemon juice or water
4 oz (100 g) butter or margarine
6 oz (150 g) self-raising flour
2 level teaspoons cocoa
½ teaspoon salt
4 oz (100 g) brown sugar
2 oz (50 g) chopped walnuts
1 large or 2 small eggs
½ level teaspoon bicarbonate of soda
4 tablespoons milk
½ teaspoon vanilla essence

1. Chop the dates and put into a small saucepan. Add water or lemon juice and the butter or margarine. Heat gently until butter

has melted and mixture comes to the boil. Remove from heat and mash well.

2. Have ready a 6½ in cake pan about 2½ in deep. If it is not non-stick, grease it well or line bottom with a round of greaseproof paper.
3. Sieve the dry ingredients, except the bicarbonate of soda into mixing bowl. Add sugar and walnuts.
4. Beat the egg or eggs in a small bowl. Dissolve the bicarbonate of soda in the milk and add.
5. Add this liquid and the date mixture to the dry ingredients with the vanilla. Mix well, but do not beat. (Flour toughens if it is beaten too much.)
6. Pour 1½ pints (¾ litre) water into pressure pan. Insert rack and begin to heat.
7. Tip mixture into cake tin. Cover with foil and secure with a rubber band or string. Lower into pressure pan. Cover with an enamel plate. Let the water boil gently without pressure for *1 hour 40 minutes.*
8. When time is up, take out the tin, remove foil, and turn the cake out after about 5 minutes.

WHOLEMEAL ONE-EGG CAKE

Time: 1½ hours *Yield: about 1½ lb or ¾ kg*

A 'nutty' textured cake with an interesting flavour.

4 oz (100 g or ⅞ cup) self-raising flour
4 oz (100 g) wholemeal flour
½ teaspoon salt
3 oz (75 g) butter or margarine
5 oz (125 g) brown sugar
1 level teaspoon mixed spice
1 large egg
¼ pint (125 ml) milk and water, half and half
½ level teaspoon bicarbonate of soda
½ teaspoon vanilla essence
4 oz (100 g) sultanas
2 oz (50 g) chopped walnuts

1. Sieve the two flours and the salt into mixing bowl. Add butter or margarine and rub in with the tips of the fingers until mixture is crumbly. Add sugar and spice, then sultanas and walnuts.
2. Have ready a cake tin about 6½ in across and 2½ in deep. If not non-stick grease well or put a round of greaseproof paper on the bottom.

3. Beat the egg in a small bowl and add milk, bicarbonate of soda and vanilla. Stir until soda has dissolved completely. Stir into the dry ingredients and mix well.
4. Pour 1½ pints (¾ litre) into pressure pan and insert rack. Begin to heat.
5. Tip mixture into cake tin, cover with foil and secure with string or a rubber band. Lower into pressure pan.
6. Cover with an enamel plate and boil gently without pressure for *1½ hours.*
7. When time is up lift out tin and remove foil, leave for about 5 minutes or longer, then turn cake out.

SULTANA ONE-EGG CAKE

Time: 1 hour 50 minutes *Yield: about 1½ lb (¾ kg)*

As this fruit cake is steamed instead of baked, it will not have its usually shiny dry top. A few minutes under the grill will help.

4 oz (100 g) sultanas
4 oz (100 g) butter or margarine
5 oz (125 g) brown sugar
½ teaspoon salt
4 tablespoons water
1 large egg
½ teaspoon each of vanilla, almond and lemon essences
7 oz (175 g) self-raising flour
½ level teaspoon cinnamon

1. Put the sultanas, butter or margarine, brown sugar, salt and water into a saucepan big enough to hold all the ingredients. This will save using a bowl. Heat, stirring well, until butter or margarine has melted. Set aside until cool, or lukewarm if you are in a hurry.
2. Have ready a cake tin about 6½ in across and 2½ in deep. If it is not non-stick, grease well or put a round of greaseproof paper on the bottom.
3. Beat the egg in a bowl and add the essences.
4. Put 1½ pints (¾ litre) water into pressure pan and insert rack. Begin to heat.
5. Sieve the flour and cinnamon into the cooled mixture, then add the beaten egg. Mix well. Tip into cake tin. Cover with foil and secure with string or a rubber band. Lower into pressure pan.

Cover with an enamel plate. Let the water boil gently without pressure for *1 hour 50 minutes.*

6. When time is up, take out tin and remove foil. Turn cake out after about 5 minutes.

CHERRY AND COCONUT CAKE

Time: 1 hour 40 minutes *Yield: about 1½ lb (¾ kg)*

The coconut improves the texture of the cake and the cherries provide the attractive dots of colour.

4 oz (100 g) butter or margarine
5 oz (125 g) sugar
1 tablespoon hot water
6 oz (150 g) self-raising flour
½ teaspoon salt
2 large eggs
2 heaped tablespoons desiccated coconut
2 oz (50 g) glacé cherries, halved
2 tablespoons milk
½ teaspoon vanilla essence

1. Put butter or margarine, sugar and hot water into mixing bowl. Beat either by hand or electric mixer until creamy.
2. Put flour and salt into sieve. Add 1 tablespoon of this to the creamed mixture, then add one of the eggs. Beat well. Add the other egg and continue to beat until light.
3. Have ready a 6½ in cake tin about 2½ in deep. If not non-stick grease well or put a round of greaseproof paper on the bottom.
4. Pour 1½ pints (¾ litre) water into pressure pan and insert rack. Begin to heat.
5. Sieve the flour into the mixture, adding the coconut, cherries, milk and vanilla. Mix well, but do not beat.
6. Pour into the cake tin. Cover with foil and secure with string or a rubber band. Lower into pressure pan. Cover with an enamel plate.
7. Let water boil gently without pressure and allow *1 hour and 40 minutes.*
8. Remove from heat, take out the tin and remove foil. Leave on cake rack for 5 minutes or longer, then turn out.

CHOCOLATE ALMOND CAKE

Time: 1½ hours *Yield: about 1¼ lb (600 g)*

4 oz (100 g) sugar
4 oz (75 g) butter or margarine
1 tablespoon hot water
5½ oz (137 g or 1 cup) self-raising flour
½ teaspoon salt
1 level tablespoon cocoa
2 large eggs
1 oz (25 g) ground almonds
5 tablespoons milk
½ teaspoon each of almond and vanilla essence

1. Put sugar and butter into mixing bowl and add the water. Beat either by hand or electric mixer until light and smooth.
2. Have ready a 6½ in cake tin about 2½ in deep. If not non-stick, grease well or line bottom with a round of grease-proof paper.
3. Sieve together the flour, salt and cocoa. Add 1 tablespoon of this to the creamed mixture then add one of the eggs. Beat well. Add the other egg and continue beating until light, adding almonds.
4. Sieve in the rest of the dry ingredients and add the milk and essences. Tip into cake tin. Cover with foil and secure with string or a rubber band.
5. Pour 1½ pints (¾ litre) water into pressure pan and insert rack. Heat.
6. Put the cake into the pressure pan and cover with an enamel plate. Bring the water to the boil then turn down the heat and let it boil gently without pressure for *1½ hours*.
7. Remove from heat, take out the tin and remove foil. Let tin stand on a cake rack for 5 minutes or longer, then turn out. Ice with chocolate icing.

SPONGE CAKE

Time: 1 hour 6 minutes

A slightly larger, taller cake than in the preceding recipe.

2 large or 3 small eggs
5 oz (125 g) sugar
3 tablespoons hot water
1 scant tablespoon golden syrup
1½ rounded tablespoons butter
2 rounded teaspoons cornflour

4½ oz (112 g) self-raising flour
½ teaspoon salt
½ teaspoon vanilla essence
whipped cream or butter filling

1. Put eggs, sugar and 1 tablespoon of the hot water into mixing bowl. Beat by hand or electric mixer until very light and foamy.
2. Have ready a 6½ in cake pan, 2½ in deep. If not non-stick, grease well or put a round of greaseproof paper on the bottom.
3. Melt in a small saucepan the golden syrup, butter or margarine with 2 tablespoons hot water.
4. Put the cornflour, flour and salt into a sieve and add alternately with the melted mixture to the beaten egg and sugar. Mix well, but do not beat. Add vanilla.
5. Put 1½ pints (¾ litre) water into pressure pan. Insert rack and begin to heat.
6. Pour cake mixture into tin. Cover with foil and secure with string or a rubber band.
7. Lower into pressure pan. Cover with an enamel plate. Let the water boil gently and *allow 1 hour and 6 minutes.*
8. Move pan from heat and take out tin. Turn out on to a cake rack. When cool, cut through horizontally and fill with slightly sweetened whipped cream with a few drops of vanilla added or a butter filling. Either ice the top or dust with icing sugar.

Chocolate sponge cake: Replace cornflour with cocoa.

Coffee sponge cake: Use strong black coffee instead of water.

NO-OVEN YEAST BREAD

Time: 1 hour 10 minutes *Yield: 3 lb*

Cooked in your pan without pressure, yeast bread is as successful as cake. The top will look pallid when it emerges, but this may be rectified by placing it under the grill.

1 oz (25 g) baker's or dried yeast
1 tablespoon sugar
about 1 pint (½ litre) lukewarm water
2 lb (1 kg) plain flour (or part wholewheat flour may be used)
2 heaped teaspoons salt

1. Put the baker's yeast into a small bowl and add the sugar. Stir until it becomes a liquid. (It will!) If dried yeast is used, soak first in 2 tablespoons lukewarm water, then add the sugar. Add 4 tablespoons lukewarm water.
2. Sieve the flour and salt into a large mixing bowl. Make a well in the centre and add yeast and sugar. When it begins to bubble, mix in the rest of the lukewarm water. Mix to a pliable dough. A little more water may be needed. The dough should not be wet, just slightly sticky.
3. Cover bowl with a towel and leave in a warmish room (not in a hot place) for about 2 hours, or until the dough has doubled in bulk. In a cool room it could be left overnight.
4. Tip dough on to a floured board and with floury hands knead for about 4 minutes. Add a little more flour if it is sticky.
5. Have ready a small well-greased loaf tin or other tin that will fit comfortably into your pressure pan, and which will allow the bread to double in size while cooking.
6. Break off about one-third of the dough and put into the tin. Cover and allow to stand until beginning to rise, about ½ hour.
7. Put 1 pint (½ litre) water into pressure pan and insert rack. Begin to heat. Cover tin with foil, making a pleat across the centre to allow for rising. Tie with string or a rubber band. Lower into pressure pan. Cover pan with an enamel plate and let the water boil gently. Simmer for 1 hour and 10 minutes.
8. Take out tin and remove foil. Remove loaf from tin and put into grilling pan, without rack, and carefully grill the top until crisp and browned. The bottom may also be browned.
9. The rest of the dough could be kept in the refrigerator. Cover completely with foil. Use when needed, either for more bread, or, if you have an oven, for rolls.

7. Sauces, Stuffings, Pastas, Pulses and Cereals

Sauces

With one exception, Caramelised Condensed Milk for Sweet Sauces (*p. 195*), the following sauces are cooked without pressure.

BASIC CREAM SAUCE

In a saucepan melt 1 rounded tablespoon butter or margarine. When sizzling, but not brown, add 1 rounded tablespoon flour. Cook these two together, still not allowing it to brown, for 2 minutes. Remove from heat. Whisk in ½ pint (¼ litre) milk or part milk and part cream, cooking until it is thick and smooth. Season with salt and pepper.

Cheese sauce: Add 2–3 oz (50–75 g) grated sharp cheese. Celery salt may replace some of the salt.

Caper sauce: Add 1 tablespoon capers and 2 teaspoons of the caper liquid from the bottle. If you are not using bottled capers, replace the liquid with vinegar.

Mustard sauce: Omit 1 tablespoon of the milk. Mix 2 teaspoons dry mustard with 1 tablespoon vinegar and 1 teaspoon sugar. When sauce has thickened, stir in the mustard mixture. Cook for another minute.

Egg sauce: Add 2 chopped hard-boiled eggs and 1 or more teaspoons chopped parsley. For a fish dish, add 1 tablespoon anchovy sauce.

CELERY SAUCE

(1) *Using packet soup:* To ½ pint (¼ litre) milk allow 1 level tablespoon celery soup powder. For a thick sauce, add an extra teaspoon of the powder. Put the cold milk into a small saucepan and add the powder. Cook and stir until thickened, then cook for about 8 minutes. If the sauce seems too salty, add 1 level teaspoon sugar.

(2) *Using fresh celery:* Wash and finely chop 3 sticks of celery. Drop into a small saucepan and add 6 tablespoons water and a little salt. Cover with lid and boil gently until soft. Add ¼ pint (125 ml) milk and 1 rounded tablespoon butter. Mix 1 level dessertspoon arrowroot or cornflour with 2 tablespoons milk until smooth. Stir into the celery mixture and cook and stir until thickened. Season with more salt and pepper: part celery or onion salt may be used.

Celery and cheese sauce: When cooked, by either method, stir in 2 or 3 oz (50–75 g) grated sharp cheese, preferably Parmesan but Cheddar would do. To add piquancy, 2 teaspoons Worcester sauce could be added.

ONION AND PARSLEY SAUCE

Peel and chop finely 1 onion. Put 1 rounded tablespoon butter in a small saucepan and heat. Add the onions and fry without browning for 5 minutes, or until transparent. Now add 1 rounded tablespoon flour and cook with the onions for 1 minute. Do not allow to brown. Remove from heat and whisk in ½ pint (¼ litre) warm milk. Return to heat and whisk and cook until smooth. Continue cooking for 2 minutes. Lastly add 1 or more teaspoons chopped parsley.

HOLLANDAISE SAUCE

Have ready a double saucepan with water boiling gently in the lower part. Into the top part put 2 egg yolks, 3 oz (75 g) butter, 2 tablespoons lemon juice, a little salt and pepper and ½ teaspoon sugar. Place on top of the lower saucepan. While the water underneath simmers gently, whisk the ingredients together until thickened. With asparagus serve lukewarm.

Note: A simpler version is given in the following recipe.

MOCK HOLLANDAISE SAUCE

Make the basic Cream Sauce (*p. 192*). Remove from heat, cool slightly, then beat in 1 whole egg, 1 tablespoon butter and 2 tablespoons lemon juice. Add ½ teaspoon sugar and season well with salt and pepper. Return to heat for 1 minute to cook through, but do not allow to boil.

BRANDY SAUCES

Traditionally served with Christmas pudding.

(*1*) **Brandy butter:** Cream together 4 oz (100 g) softened butter with 4 oz (100 g) icing or castor sugar, then add 1 or 2 tablespoons brandy. Put into refrigerator or cool place until firm.

(*2*) **Brandy sauce:** Make basic Cream Sauce (*p. 192*), then add 1 level tablespoon brown sugar and brandy to taste.

HARD SAUCE

This is a non-alcoholic sauce to accompany steamed puddings. Cream together 4 oz (100 g) softened butter with 4 oz (100 g) icing sugar then add ½ teaspoon vanilla essence, a pinch of cinnamon and 2 or 3 teaspoons of lemon juice. Add the grated rind of the lemon if possible.

CUMBERLAND SAUCE

Into a saucepan put 3 tablespoons redcurrant jelly, the grated rind and juice of 1 large orange, and 4 tablespoons port wine or a sweet sherry. Begin to heat. Mix 1 level tablespoon arrowroot with 2 tablespoons water and stir in. Cook until thickened, stirring constantly. Cover with lid until needed to prevent a skin forming. If liked, a little cream may be added.

SWEET-SOUR SAUCE

Melt 2 level tablespoons butter or margarine in a small saucepan. Add 2 level tablespoons flour. Stir and cook without browning for 2 minutes. Remove from heat and add 1½ gills (188 ml) stock, or water with a chicken stock cube, 2 tablespoons vinegar or lemon juice, 2 tablespoons brown sugar, 2 teaspoons soy sauce, 1 tablespoon sweet chutney and a dash of pepper. Return to heat and whisk and cook until smooth and thick. If unseasoned stock is used, add salt to taste. If the cube is used, it should provide, with the soy sauce, enough salt. Lastly add about 4 tablespoons cream.

Note: If this is made for small beetroot, some of the liquor in which the beetroot has been cooked could replace half the stock or water.

TOMATO SAUCE (*p. 68, step 2*)

SAVOURY TOMATO SAUCE (*p. 128*)

CARAMELISED CONDENSED MILK FOR SWEET SAUCES

The pressure saucepan will do this job in half the time needed in an ordinary saucepan.

Put 2 or 3 medium-sized cans of sweetened condensed milk on the rack in the pressure pan. Pour in 2 pints (1 litre) water. Fix lid and bring to pressure. *Allow 1½ hours.* When opened the condensed milk will be a caramel colour and have a delicious caramel taste. To use as a sweet sauce, thin with water or milk and add a few drops of vanilla essence. Rum or brandy may be added instead of some of the milk or water. The tins, unopened, will keep for years.

In an ordinary saucepan boil for 3 hours.

Stuffings (without pressure)

FORCEMEAT STUFFING

Sufficient for a 2½–3½ lb (1¼–1¾ kg) chicken.

Combine 3 oz (75 g or 1½ cups) fresh breadcrumbs with ½ teaspoon dried thyme or mixed herbs, 1 small grated onion, a little chopped parsley, ½ teaspoon salt and a dash of pepper. Chop in roughly 2 teaspoons butter or margarine. Do not add an egg or any liquid.

RICE, MUSHROOM AND PRUNE STUFFING

Sufficient for a chicken as in previous recipe.

Combine 6 oz (150 g or 1 cup) cooked rice with 2 oz (50 g) mushrooms, previously fried in a little butter and cut into pieces, and ½ cup cooked chopped prunes. Add ½ teaspoon dried thyme or mixed herbs and season with salt and pepper.

CHESTNUT STUFFING

Sufficient to stuff a medium-sized turkey.

Although there are no roast turkey recipes in this book, the chestnuts can be so quickly prepared in a pressure pan that it seemed a good idea to include this stuffing.

Prepare 1 lb (½ kg) chestnuts as directed on *p. 38*. Remove outer and inner skins and either pulverise in your electric blender or mash with a fork. Mix with 4 oz (100 g or 2 cups) fresh breadcrumbs, 1 teaspoon dried thyme, 2 grated onions, 1 level teaspoon salt and a little pepper. Chop in roughly 4 teaspoons butter. Chopped parsley may be added. Do not add an egg or any liquid.

BACON, APPLE AND ONION STUFFING

Remove rinds from 2 rashers of bacon. Cut into ½ in pieces and fry until crisp. Tip into a bowl. Add 4 oz (100 g or 2 cups) fresh breadcrumbs, 1 medium-sized grated onion, and 1 or 2 peeled and grated sweet apples. Add ½ teaspoon salt, 1 teaspoon sugar and a little pepper. Chop in 2 teaspoons butter. Chopped parsley may be added. Do not add any egg or liquid.

Pasta, Pulses and Cereals
(Pressure-cooked)

Barley: To 8 oz (¼ kg) pearl barley, allow 1½ pints (¾ litre) water and 1 level teaspoon salt. Fix lid and bring to pressure. *Allow 20 minutes.*

Beans, haricot, butter, lima etc.: To 8 oz (¼ kg) beans allow 2 pints (1 litre) water and 2 level teaspoons salt. Soak for 4 hours or overnight. Fix lid and bring to pressure. *Allow 30 minutes.*

Lentils: To 8 oz (¼ kg) lentils, allow 2½ pints (1¼ litres) water. Add 1 teaspoon salt. Fix lid and bring to pressure. *Allow 12 minutes.*

Macaroni: To 6 oz (150 g) macaroni allow 2 pints (1 litre) water and 1 level teaspoon salt. Fix lid and bring to pressure. *Allow 9 minutes.* 5 minutes for quick-cooking varieties.

Noodles: To 3 oz (75 g) noodles allow 2½ pints (1¼ litres) water and 1 level teaspoon salt. Fix lid and bring to pressure. *Allow 3 minutes.*

Peas, dried, green, whole: To 8 oz (¼ kg) peas allow 2½ pints (1¼ litres) water and 1 level teaspoon salt. Fix lid and bring to pressure. *Allow 25 minutes.*

Peas, pink, split: To 8 oz (¼ kg) peas allow 2½ pints (1¼ litres) water and 1 level teaspoon salt. Fix lid and bring to pressure. *Allow 15 minutes, 22 minutes for soup.*

Porridge: For coarse oatmeal *allow 4 minutes.* For fine, *allow 3 minutes.*

Rice: To 8 oz (¼ kg or 1 cup) uncooked rice, allow 1½ pints (¾ litre) water and 1 teaspoon salt. Fix lid and bring to pressure. *Allow 3 minutes for long-grain rice, 4 minutes for pudding rice and 5 minutes for natural brown rice,* tip into a strainer and rinse under the tap. To reheat, either toss in butter or oil in the pressure pan or steam in the strainer over hot water for a few minutes.

Spaghetti: As for macaroni, but *allow 8 minutes.*

Vermicelli: As for macaroni, but *allow 6 minutes.*

8. Jam, Marmalade and Preserving

Jam and Marmalade

The advantages of pressure-cooking in this field are two-fold. *First*, the preliminary cooking of marmalade and some jams is done in one-quarter of the time, and *second*, the final quick boil after the sugar has been added benefits from the base of the pressure pan which is so much heavier than that of most ordinary saucepans. The rolling boil is even and consistent and burning is less likely.

Because no preliminary process is necessary when using soft fruits such as berries, these recipes have been eliminated. In these cases, just use your pressure pan as an ordinary saucepan.

Before beginning preparations, put the jars into a slow oven to sterilise and become hot.

Testing: Put 1 teaspoon of the jam or marmalade on a cool saucer and leave for 5 seconds. Now hold it so that the light falls on the surface of the syrup and move the finger gently over it. If it wrinkles, showing that a skin has formed, the jam or marmalade is ready to be put into jars. Another test is to lift the spoon and watch how the drops fall. If in heavy blobs it is a sign that it will jell.

Bottling: Pour jams and marmalades whilst still hot into warm jars, cover at once with wax discs. When cold, put on cellophane covers.

ORANGE MARMALADE (1)

Pressure-cooking time: 8 minutes *Yield: about 4½ lb or 2¼ kg*

1½ lb (¾ kg) Seville oranges
1½ pints (¾ litre) water
2 lemons
3 lb (1½ kg) sugar

1. Slice the oranges finely and put into pressure pan, without rack or trivet. Add the water.
2. Fix lid and bring to pressure. *Allow 8 minutes.*
3. Reduce pressure and remove lid.
4. Add the juice and grated rind of the lemons and the sugar. Stir until sugar has dissolved, then bring to the boil, uncovered, and boil with a good rolling boil for about 30 minutes or until the marmalade responds to the test.

ORANGE MARMALADE (2)

Pressure-cooking time: 10 minutes *Yield as above*

Here the oranges are boiled whole first, then minced or cut into chunky pieces. Only the rind is softened.

Ingredients exactly as for Orange Marmalade (1)

1. Cut the oranges in halves. Remove pips and put them into a piece of muslin and tie with thread.
2. Pour water into pressure pan without trivet or rack. Add the halved oranges. Fix lid and bring to pressure. *Allow 3 minutes.*
3. Reduce pressure and remove lid.
4. Lift out the oranges and leave the water in the pan. Either mince the oranges, or cut into chunky pieces. Put back into pan with the muslin bag. Fix lid and bring to pressure. *Allow 7 minutes.*
5. Reduce pressure and remove lid. Lift out bag and add the sugar and lemons. Proceed then as step 4 in preceding recipe.

MELON AND PINEAPPLE JAM

Pressure-cooking time: 10 minutes *Yield: about 4 lb (2 kg)*

2 lb (1 kg) melon, weighed after peeling and removing seeds
¼ pint (125 ml) lemon juice
2 lb (1 kg) sugar
a large 29 oz (725 g approx.) can of pineapple chunks, or a 2½ lb fresh pineapple

1. Cut melon into small cubes and put into pressure pan. Add lemon juice and ¼ pint (125 ml) pineapple syrup or juice. Fix lid and bring to pressure. *Allow 10 minutes.*
2. Reduce pressure and remove lid. Add sugar and stir until it dissolves before heating again.
3. Add the chopped pineapple. Bring to the boil and boil with a good rolling boil until jam is golden and thick and responds to the test.

PINEAPPLE AND DRIED APRICOT JAM

Pressure-cooking time: 12 minutes *Yield: about 6 lb (3 kg)*

1 lb (½ kg) dried apricots
2 large 29 oz (725 g approx.) cans pineapple chunks, or 2 large fresh pineapples
3 lb (1½ kg) sugar

1. Open cans, or peel, core and cut up the fresh pineapple. Measure syrup or juice and make up to 2 pints (1 litre) with water.
2. Pour into pressure pan. Wash apricots, cut in halves with scissors and add. Allow to soak for 20 minutes or longer.
3. Fix lid and bring to pressure. *Allow 12 minutes.*
4. Reduce pressure and remove lid. Add chopped pineapple and sugar. Stir until dissolved then bring to the boil and boil with a good rolling boil until jam is thick and responds to the test.

DRIED APRICOT JAM

Pressure-cooking time: 12 minutes *Yield: about 4½ lb (2¼ kg)*

1 lb (½ kg) dried apricots
2½ pints (1¼ litres) water
3½ lb (1¾ kg) sugar

1. Put apricots and water into pressure pan. Fix lid and bring to pressure. *Allow 12 minutes.*
2. Reduce pressure and remove lid.
3. Add the sugar. Stir until it dissolves then boil briskly with a good rolling boil until jam is thick and responds to the test.

Dried apricot jam with orange juice: Replace ½ pint (¼ litre) of the water with orange juice. Add also the grated rinds.

MIXED DRIED FRUIT JAM

Pressure-cooking time: 12 minutes *Yield: about 5 lb (2½ kg approx.)*

Mixtures of dried fruits such as apricots, prunes, peaches and pears may often be bought all together in a packet. If not, choose your own mixture. Just prunes and apricots, ½ lb (¼ kg) of each, will make a fine jam.

1 lb (½ kg) mixed dried fruits
2 pints (1 litre) water
juice of 1 large lemon
3½ lb (1¾ kg) sugar

1. Wash and cut up the fruits with scissors. Put into pressure pan and add the water. Allow to soak for about 20 minutes.
2. Fix lid and bring to pressure. *Allow 12 minutes.*
3. Reduce pressure and remove lid.
4. Stir in lemon and sugar. Stir until dissolved then bring to the boil and boil with a good rolling boil until thick.

GOOSEBERRY JAM

Pressure-cooking time: 5 minutes *Yield: 5 lb (2½ kg) approx.*

2 lb (1 kg) gooseberries, preferably green
2 pints (1 litre) water
3½ lb (1¾ kg) sugar

1. Top and tail gooseberries. Wash and put into pressure pan. Add the water.
2. Fix lid and bring to pressure. *Allow 5 minutes.*
3. Reduce pressure and remove lid. Add sugar. Stir until sugar has dissolved then bring to the boil and boil with a good rolling boil until it responds to test.

QUINCE JAM

Pressure-cooking time: 15 minutes *Yield: about 4½ lb (2¼ kg)*

2 lb (1 kg) quinces
¾ pint (375 ml) water
an extra pint water (½ litre)
juice of one large lemon
2½ lb (1¼ kg) sugar

1. Peel and core the quinces. Cut each into eight pieces and place in pressure pan. Add the ¾ pint water and fix lid. Bring to pressure and *allow 15 minutes.*
2. Put peelings and cores into another saucepan with the additional 1 pint water and the lemon juice. Boil gently for 10 minutes.
3. Reduce pressure and remove lid. Add the sugar and the strained juice from the cores etc. Stir until sugar has dissolved then bring to the boil and boil with a good rolling boil until jam responds to test.

Preserving

Many people are persuaded to buy a High Dome or other large-sized pressure pan in case they should wish to use it to preserve their fruits and vegetables. These pans are useful for this purpose and will take the taller quart (litre) jars. Remember though that the weight of the pan, plus the High Dome and the bottles and contents, will be considerable. Smaller-sized pressure pans may also be used for preserving and will take the pint (½ litre) sized jars. For small families this could be the best type of jar to use.

The question to be pondered therefore when considering a pressure pan purchase, is whether it is worth while to suffer the added weight of the High Dome for everyday use just for the sake of a few weeks' bottling in the summer.

GENERAL DIRECTIONS FOR PRESERVING FRUITS

1. See that the jars are clean and in perfect condition. Examine them carefully for cracks or nicks.
2. Keep the jars warm, either by standing them in hot water or putting them into a slow oven.
3. Try the jars in your pressure pan. There should be about ¼ in between them to allow the steam to circulate. You should get three of the narrower jars or two of the fatter types in an average sized pan.

4. Be sure that the fruit is firm, preferably just ripe and with no blemishes.
5. Boil up the syrup in a separate pan, using the quantities of sugar and water suggested for each type of fruit.
6. Fill the warm jars with the fruit, packing as *tightly as possible.* This will prevent the fruit from rising in the jars.
7. Put 1½ pints (¾ litre) water into pressure pan and insert rack or trivet. Add a little acid (*see p. 17*).
8. Pour the hot syrup into the fruit-filled jars, filling up to within ½ in from the top.
9. Adjust the lids. With self-sealing tops, put them on and adjust the screw band. Screw down tightly then unscrew half a turn. Lids with rubber bands should also be screwed down tightly then unscrewed one turn backwards. This allows for expansion and also lets any remaining air out that might remain in the jars. Clips should also be adjusted.
10. Place jars in the pressure pan.
11. Fix lid and *bring only to 5 lb pressure* (*low*). Allow times given in the table following.
12. Turn off heat and let the pressure reduce gradually. *Do not cool with cold water.*
13. Lift weight from pan and remove lid. Have a double thickness of towelling ready for the jars. Holding a small towel, lift the jars on to the towelling.
14. For both types of screw tops, screw down tightly. After 10 minutes, screw again.
15. After 24 hours test the covers. If they will lift off, either use the fruit at once or process again.

TABLES FOR PRESERVING FRUITS

Preparation	Syrup	Timing
Apples, peel and cut into ⅛ in slices, removing core. Put into salted water while preparing to prevent darkening.	Syrup of 1 pint (½ litre) water to ½ lb (¼ kg) sugar.	Process for *8 minutes* at 5 lb pressure (low) for eating apples, *5 minutes* for cooking apples.
Apricots, wash but do not peel. Leave whole unless large ones.	Syrup of 1 pint (½ litre) water to ½ lb (¼ kg) sugar.	Process for *5 minutes* at 5 lb pressure (low).
Berries (blackberries, strawberries, raspberries, etc.), remove any bits of stem or leaf. Place in a large bowl.	Tip the sugar over the berries. Use 6 oz (150 g) for each 1 lb (½ kg) of berries. Add also ¼ pint (125 ml) water for each 2 lb (1 kg) berries. Allow to stand until sugar melts and forms a rich syrup. Strain the syrup off into a saucepan and bring to the boil, then proceed as in *step 8*.	Process for *3 minutes* at 5 lb pressure (low).
Cherries, remove stems and wash.	Syrup of 1½ pints (¾ litre) water to ½ lb (¼ kg) sugar.	Process for *3 minutes* at 5 lb pressure (low).
Peaches, either peel or rub over with an abrasive pad. Halve and remove stones.	Syrup of 1 pint (½ litre) water with ½ lb (¼ kg) sugar.	Process for *10 minutes* at 5 lb pressure (low).
Pears, peel, halve, core and cut into quarters or eighths.	Syrup of 1 pint (½ litre) water and ½ lb (¼ kg) sugar.	Process for *10 minutes* at 5 lb pressure (low) if hard, *8 minutes*, if firm but ripe.
Plums, wash and remove stems.	Syrup of 1 pint (½ litre) water to ½ lb (¼ kg) sugar.	Process for *3 minutes* at 5 lb pressure (low).

Preparation	Syrup	Timing
Rhubarb, wash sticks and cut into ½ in pieces.	Syrup of 1 pint (½ litre) water to ¾ lb (375 g) sugar.	Process for *3 minutes* at 5 lb pressure (low) if garden variety, *1 minute* if forced.
Tomatoes, remove skins and stem ends. Use firm ripe tomatoes only.	1 level tablespoon sugar and 1 rounded teaspoon salt to 2 pints (1 litre) water.	Process for *8 minutes* at 5 lb pressure (low).

Index